My Best RV

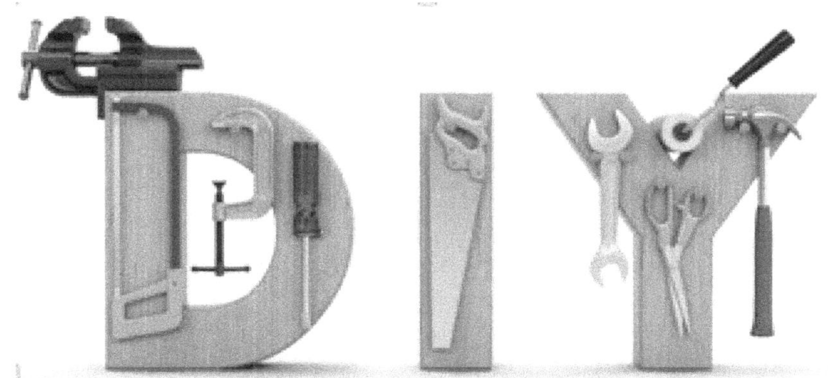

Projects

By James Edward Clicquennoi

Dedicated to My Wife who has put up with my RV hobby for the past thirty three years and supported me when I made the huge leap into a motorhome.

Read my other books

"RV TWEAKS MODIFICATIONS and UPGRADES Volume II"

"Motorhome Maintenance DIY and Save"

available at www.Amazon.com.

Table of Contents

INTRODUCTION

This is by far my best book yet. It is packed with 37 DIY projects that you the reader have asked for and can easily performing with the given information.

Last year as I traveled around the US I asked fellow campers what their issues were, what were their wants, and desires for their RVs. Many wanted more storage in one form or another. Some wanted solar but did not understand the concepts or where to begin. Everyone with a residential refrigerator wanted to know how to keep the door from coming open when traveling. In the summer months they wanted to cool the inside of their RV without having to constantly run the air conditioners. One big item was an affordable key less entry and of course ideas to make their RV Life easier.

I took notes, did my research, and the result is this book, "My Best RV DIY Projects". I hope you enjoy reading it as much as I enjoyed researching and writing it.

.

Did you know that if you drive a diesel pusher motorhome you have built in auxiliary air supply or compressor? That is right. The compressor that is used to air up the chassis or supply the air breaks has a port for the user to tap into to do such things as blow up tires, run air horns or other accessories that need compressed air. The supply tops out at 120psi.

For those using it to blow up motorhome tires you need to catch the compressor at the max pressure. To accomplish this have the diesel engine running and bleed off enough air so the compressor kicks in, then begin airing your tires.

The user port where you tap in should appear as in the picture. This is the only approved location as it is fed by a line with a back flow control valve. This means that if anything were to go wrong with whatever you connect into the air system it will not affect your breaks or suspension.

This manifold can often be found mounted to the cab firewall in the generator compartment. I have also seen it in the fuse bay front basement compartment on the driver's side of the coach.

Most people will attach a quick disconnect to the manifold that facilities the easy attachment of an air hose. One issue with this is the 120psi pressure. When disconnecting the air hose the high pressure can cause the hose to shoot out and injure someone. For this reason I have installed a shutoff on my manifold just before to the quick disconnect. I got both the shutoff and quick disconnect from Harbor Freight.

The shutoff I used is a ¼ inch Port Ball Valve which does not require an adaptor to screw into the manifold. Cost only about $4.00. The quick disconnect is a ¼ inch Male Brass Industrial Coupler and sells for about $4.50.

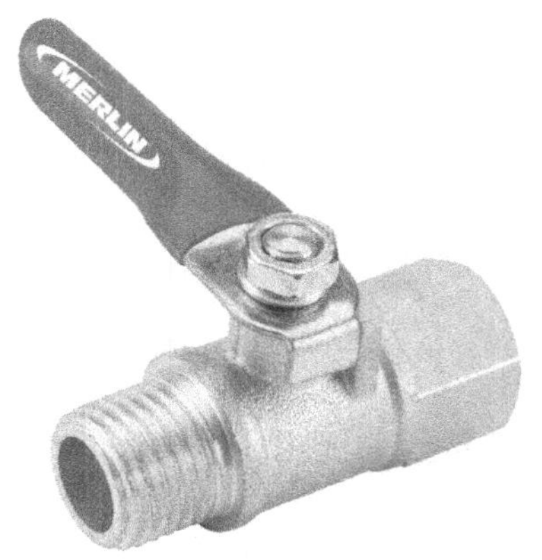

https://www.harborfreight.com/14-ifull-port-ball-valve-63553.html

https://www.harborfreight.com/14-in-male-brass-industrial-coupler-63558.html

One major improvement I have seen built into RVs over the years is the inclusion of a real bed rather than the fold down sofa bed that was popular back in the 1960s. If you have not enjoyed the fold down bed very few were comfortable leaving one sleeping on mattress cracks and waking tired and with a backache.

While the real bed is great many manufadturers install them with no side tables or side tables that are so small they will not even accommodate an alarm clock. We need a bedside end table!

Here is an idea. Make a trip out to your local Ikea store and pick up a couple of wooden magazine file holders. Finish them to match your RV's interior and mount them sideways to the wall on each side of the bed. You now have an attractive side table as well as a cubby to keep things in.

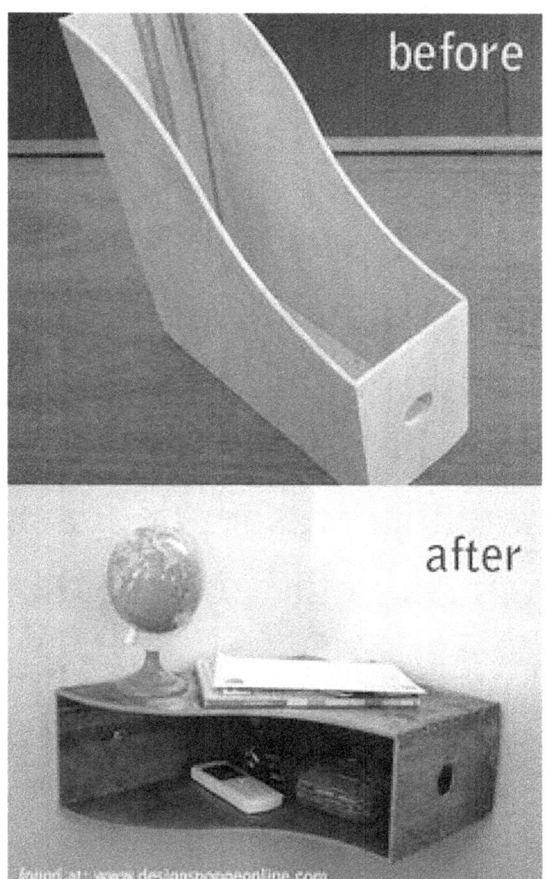

11

You could also use this idea in any corner where you would like a small shelf.

You can get two of these boxes for as little as $10.00. The following link is for a set of nesting boxes from Ikea.

http://www.ikea.com/us/en/catalog/products/50187340/?query=Magazine+File+wood

I know what you are thinking. I have these great side tables but how am I going to attach then to the thin RV walls.

Here I will take a page from the solar industry and attached the end tables using "well nuts". They can hold almost anything to the thinnest of materials. Well nuts can be found in the specialty section of the large box stores. See picture.

To use well nuts you drill a hole large enough for the rubber of the nut to fit through. Insert the nut into the hole and with a bolt about ¼ inch longer than the rubber well nut and a one inch fender washer to attach the shelf. The well nut will compress in the hole holding the shelf secure.

Below is a nice graphic showing how well nuts work. I have used these all over the RV with great success.

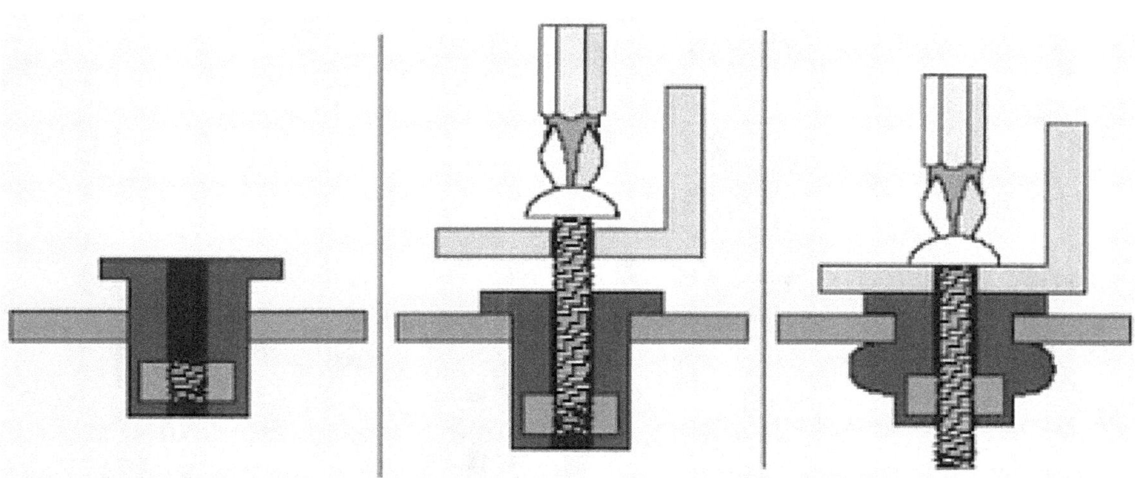

Place Well-Nut insert all the way into pre-drilled hole until flange is firmly against mounting surface.

2. Pass machine screw through part to be fastened.

3. Tighten until snug.

BATTERY MONITOR, DIGITAL AMMETER / VOLTMETER

If you have an RV I am sure that it has an onboard battery. If you do a lot of boon docking it is important to monitor that battery's health. A battery that has been discharged below 12.1 volts DC numerous times will soon suffer a premature

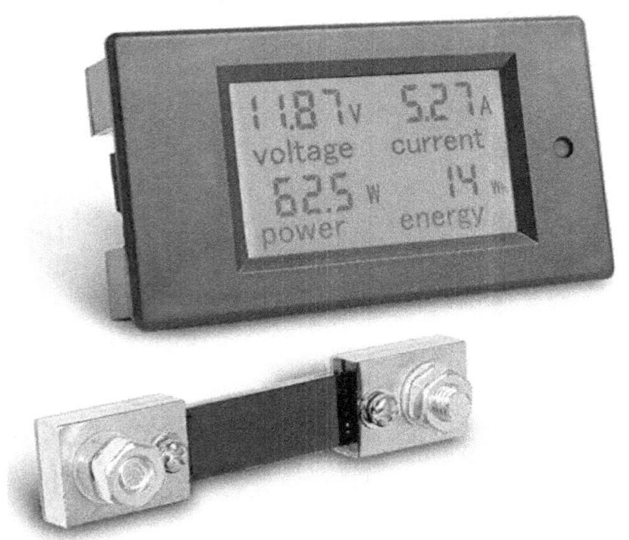

death. I had a buddy that was concerned about this and wanted to know if there was an easy way to monitor his battery's status. He was looking for a cost effective solution, not one that costs hundreds of dollars. What we found was the "MICTUNING DC 6.5-100V 0-100A LCD Digital Display Ammeter Voltmeter Multimeter Volt Watt Power Energy Meter Blue with 100A/75mV Shunt" at a cost of just $16.99.

Benefits of this meter are:

- It monitors Voltage, Current, Power and Energy measurement in one combo, super compact and lightweight unit with an easy to read digital display.

- It comes with its own shunt rated at 100 amps
- Can be programmed to any desired threshold voltage from 6.5 volts DC to 90 volts DC
- When programmed voltage threshold is reached the device comes to life and flashes the measurement and units backlight as warning.
- It can be installed to monitor battery charge or discharge. In our case we wanted discharge
- Simple to install.

There is only one caution to be aware of when doing the install. The 100 amp shunt must be electrically isolated from chassis ground. For our installation we mounted the shunt to a piece of PVC material that was

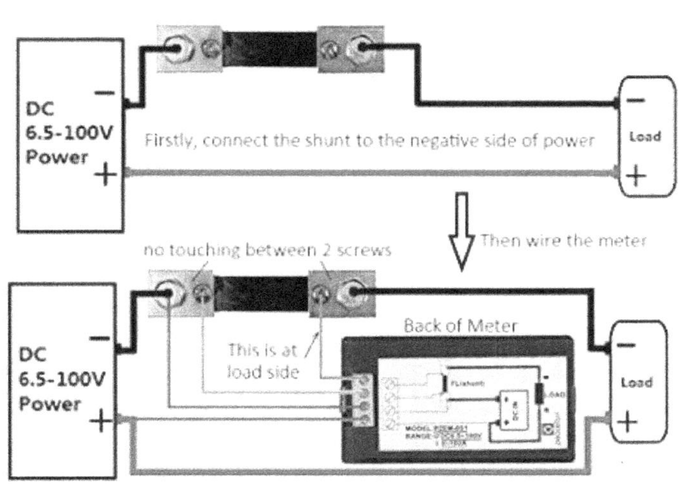

then mounted into the battery compartment. Wires were run from the battery compartment to the location on a side wall where we choose to mount the meter. The whole process including cutting the meter mounting hole took just under two hours.

Below are pictures of the installation.

If you would like to try this yourself it can be found on Amazon at the following address:

https://www.amazon.com/MICTUNING-6-5-100V-Digital-Voltmeter-Multimeter/dp/B01JOUZELG/ref=sr_1_1?ie=UTF8&qid=1529080437&sr=8-1&keywords=mictuning+ammeter

Now that fall is here I suspect you have put your RV away for the winter unless you are one of our lucky snow birds. But what to do about the RV battery? I have used two of these battery tenders for the past several

years to keep my batteries fresh through the winter months. I have one connected to my bank of four coach 6 volt batteries and one connected to my bank of two 12 volt chassis batteries and they work great. All I do is be sure to top off the battery water and plug them in. I am set for the winter. A plus with these is you can keep them connected through the summer months when you are using the RV and they do not interfere with your on board battery charger. They are a no muss no fuss solution. Harbor Freight has them on sale now for $19.98. This is a great price for a battery charger/tender.

You can find them here https://www.harborfreight.com/15-amp-three-stage-onboard-battery-charger-maintainer-99857.html

"1.5 Amp Three Stage Onboard 12V Battery Charger/Maintainer"

Recharge batteries up to three times faster than conventional units with this three-stage, fully automatic battery charger. This high frequency battery charger uses the latest technology to prolong battery life and is great for maintaining batteries while in storage. The battery charger is equipped with overload protection, short circuit protection and reverse polarity protection for added safety. LED charge indicators let you know when your battery is charged

- Charge or maintain 12 volt batteries or 6 volt batteries connected in series
- Three-stage fully automatic charge controller protects and prolongs battery life
- Automatically switches to trickle charging to prevent overcharging
- Bracket for permanent mounting in battery bay
- LED charge indicators show status at a glance

The family of this idea did not have any draws or closets in their RV bedroom. They did have a huge unused space under the bed as many of us do. They thought, how can I use this space to solve my problem? The solution was to go to Walmart and purchase a small drawer unit. They then removed the end piece of the bed support and placed the drawer unit under the bed at the foot end. Problem solved, and they still had the under bed storage for other items.

Now this is a nice solution, looks factory installed and placing it at the foot of the bed makes for easy access.

BOTTLED WATER

Here is an idea to kick around. A lot of RVers do not like to drink campground water or water from their on board storage tanks. What they do is carry bottled water. The problem is where you store it and how many gallons to bring.

Here is a slick solution I saw where the RVer installed a hand pump and put large bubbler bottles in their basement. The pump and bottles are connected with a short length of RV quality water hose. To change bottles just insert the hose into a new bottle. Use a bungee cord to secure the bottles while traveling.

Installing a hand pump rather than an electric pump will insure the bottle water is not wasted but used only for drinking and cooking. What do you think? You could also put the bottled water under the sink if there is room.

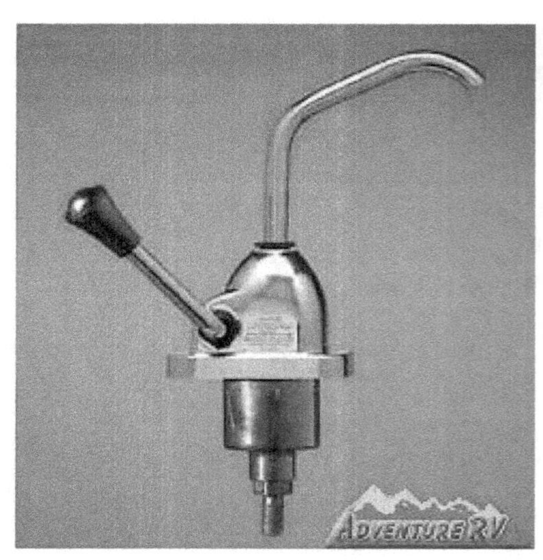

BREAD BOX CORNER SHELF

Have you got one of those corners in your RV that just seems to be empty? It is as if the RV manufacture did not know what to do with the space or just cheaped out and left it unfinished. These spaces are often found in the corner of bedroom or in the bathroom over the toilet. Well here is a solution. Build a Bread Box nook/shelf combination.

You can stain them the color of your RV interior or get creative as in the picture with colors.

Mounted on their side gives you both a shelf and nook to put things in. You could mount one on each wall over the toilet or have several mounted up the wall as pictured to the right.

I found a bread box here for only $30.00.

https://www.amazon.com/Lipper-International-8846-Bamboo-Rolltop/dp/B001GS8NX6/ref=sr_1_13?s=kitchen&ie=UTF8&qid=1516392144&sr=1-13&keywords=bread+box

You can also find different styles of Bread Boxes at WayFare. See below:

https://www.wayfair.com/kitchen-tabletop/pdp/rebrilliant-roll-top-bread-box-rebr4772.html

https://www.wayfair.com/kitchen-tabletop/pdp/lipper-international-bamboo-roll-top-bread-box-ig1623.html

Since the installation on my system several years ago the task has been made much easier with the advent of complete kits. When I did my install I had to build the kit from scratch. To follow are two of the new kits available followed by my install experience.

The first "Wen&Cheng 4CH 720P Mobile AHD DVR Realtime Video/Audio Recorder with Remote Control + 4 pcs Sony CCD Lens 130MP Camera (Black) + 4pcs Cables for Car Bus Truck Black Box Security Surveillance System"

https://www.amazon.com/Wen-Cheng-Realtime-Recorder-Surveillance/dp/B06XQSS3C2/ref=sr_1_3?s=electronics&ie=UTF8&qid=1544233246&sr=1-3&keywords=bus+dvr+systems

The second "Camnex Car Backup Camera System 9" Monitor Build-in DVR Recorder with Quad Split Screen Rear View Camera System Kit for Truck Van Caravan Trailers Camper Bus RV Harvester"

https://www.amazon.com/Camnex-Monitor-Recorder-Trailers-Harvester/dp/B073WVJ83P/ref=sr_1_4?s=electronics&ie=UTF8&qid=1544233246&sr=1-4&keywords=bus+dvr+systems

This was by far the most technical challenging and time consuming upgrade I have performed. It took two weeks to complete.

My trip to UTAH highlighted the need for some kind of camera system while driving. On the two lane highways out west there are so many drivers that will pull out to pass then wait for the last minute to get back to their lane. Additionally, RVs are always being cut off. While a dash cam is one solution it will not capture activity behind you or on your side. I felt these views were equally as important as the front view. This is why I went with a CCTV system with the four channel DVR over a simple dash cam. While driving I can record everything, 360 degrees around me. As a bonus I can use the system while parked as a security system.

My system will record 62 hours of video and audio on one SIM card.

Back in 2014 when I installed this system there were not too many around, so I had to configure it myself. Today you can purchase complete packages for as little as $300.00 to $400.00. You will want to search the internet for Bus DVR systems.

One The components I choose for my system were the DVR unit itself. "CCTV 4CH ReaMini ltime SD Card Mobile Bus Car Vehicle DVR Recorder System Audio".

Not only will this unit act as a recorder but if you wish you can set up triggers to your directional lights and backup light switch so the views on the monitor will change automatically.

I chose a system that used a SIM card to store the video rather than hard drive . I was concerned what road vibrations might do to the hard drive. If choosing today I would get one that did support a hard drive for storage and install an SSD drive. A configuration with an SSD drive could store months of video versis my 62 hours and no vibration issues.

I chose a 11 inch monitor that turns itself on when it senses power (key on). The big reason for the large size is I keep all four cameras displaied while driving.

While I did not choose these cameras but if specifing today I would. "CAIRUTE® Universal Mini CCD High Definition Night Vision 360 Degree Car Rear Front Side View Backup Camera With Mirror Image Conversion Lines"

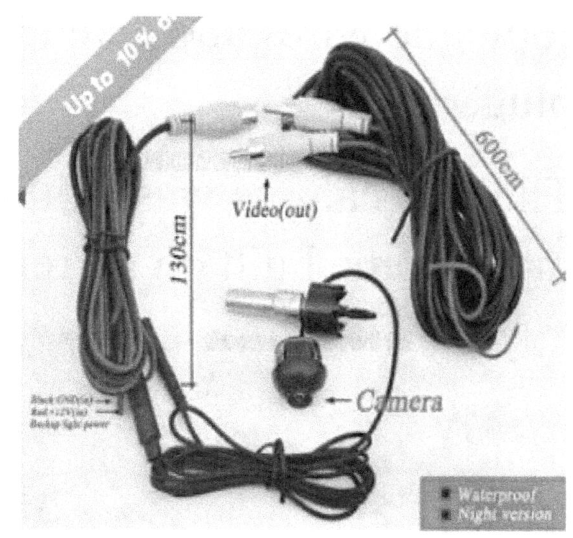

The cameras are the same form factor and specifications as I have but have the added ability to mirror the image. This is importanf as the two side cameras and back camera need to be on mirror mode. For that I needed different cameras. The cameras come with a hole saw so the mounting hole is perfict.

The microphone is "Outdoor Waterproof Adjustable Sensibility Audio Pickup Advanced Mic for DVR" This is mounted in at the front of the coach to catch any conversations.

"Car Boat SPST Blue LED Light 12V 20A Tip Toggle ON/OFF Switch" Lighted switch to turn the system on and off.

Mounting the hardware at the front of the coach was straight forward. Select a location for the cameras and microphone drill holes using the provided hole saw and mount the hardware. By opening the generator compartment I could easily route the wires and take them into the cab through a firewall plug.

The rear camera was a little more work. I have a diesel pusher motorhome built on a Freightliner XC chassis.

Down the side of each rail on this chassis are routing troths that Freightliner use to route wires and hoses from the front to back of the coach. Using an electrical snake I routed a length of 16 gauge speaker wire the length of the coach. I would like to note that anytime I route wires through the coach I also parallel a run of mason twine. This is a very strong string. I do this so if in the future I need another wire run the same place I do not have to re-snake it. I took the speaker wire and wove it along the hinge on the back engine hatch so that I could open it with the camera in place. I then chose a location for the camera, drilled the hole, mounted and connected the wires.

Inside the coach I mounted the DVR under the dash. The instructions call for the DVR to be connected to a constant power line and the ignition. I connected the DVR through the optional switch to power and used my radio power switch to simulate the ignition. This allows me to run the system while parked as well as driving.

To follow are pictures of the installation.

First, the monitor showing the four views then the DVR and the camera mounts. Note: the side cameras are mounted to shoot under the slides when they are extended and the back camera will function with the engine hatch open or closed.

31

Next a view of the DEV installed and the lighted power switch.

The front camera is mounted in the nose of the coach, just below the center of the windshield.

The side cameras are the small buttons below the side dash system cameras.

Last, the rear camera. I mounted it on the hatch so it will function with the hatch open or closed.

CENTRAL VACUUM WITH "VROOM" OPTION

I was sitting at home shortly after Christmas going through my emails when I saw one from RVupgradestore.com. I have purchased from this store in the past with good luck but it had been a long time ago. This email was promoting a Dirt Devil CV 1500 with the VROOM option. I have looked at central vacuums in the past but always decided against them because by the time I found a storage area for the 35 foot hose, the various tools, and a location for the Dirt Devil CV 1500 I could just as easily store and use the nice Shark vacuum the wife purchased.

The VROOM option caught my interest and I wondered what it was so off to www. RVupgradestore.com I went to find out. There I found a link to a YouTube video that explained the option and showed it in action. It turns out the VROOM option is a method to automatically store the 35 foot vacuum hose in the wall of the RV. Yes I said automatically. The way this works is there is a larger diameter hose that the vacuum hose fits into. This larger hose can be installed under a sink basin, in the basement, or in a hollow wall of the RV. When you want to vacuum you just pull out the inner hose to its stop, attach the wand, the attachment of choice and vacuum. When the job is complete remove the wand, place your hand over the hose and it sucks back into its storage location. For me this was a game changer. After consulting with the wife or boss as she likes to be known I purchased the unit for a spring install.

 The first and second picture shows the hardware for the CV 1500 and VROOM. I might add it was all on sale for $299.00 which made the purchase even nicer.

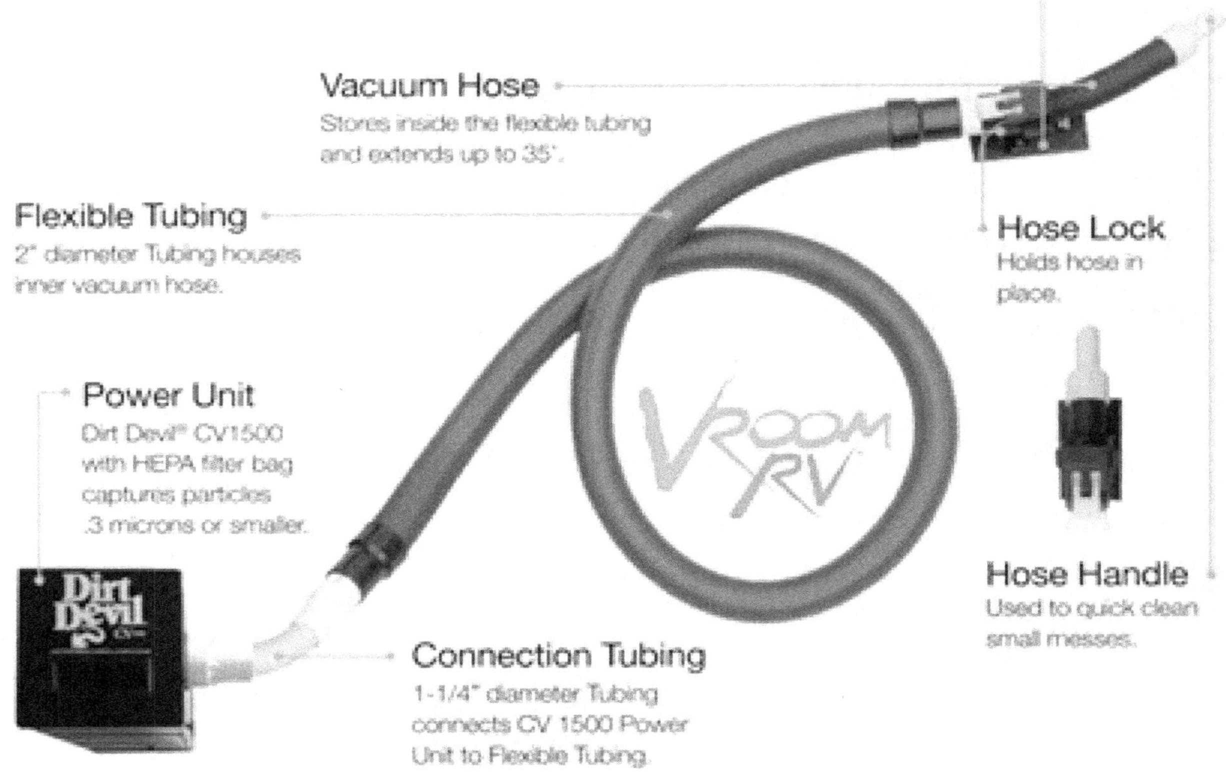

I choose to put my install under the kitchen sink. I choose this location because it is in the center of the RV so the vacuum hose easily reaches to the back and front of the RV. I also had a large blocked off space next to the hot water unit that accommodated the Dirt Devil CV 1500. I wrapped the storage hose around the kitchen sink basin attaching it with tie wraps to the clips holding the sink to the counter.   The access to the hose and on/off switch I mounted just behind the cupboard door.   I mounted the vacuum three inches above the bottom of the hot water heater in the event there was ever a water leak it would not get flooded.   The final need was a location for the vacuum tools which I am storing in a custom rack I made that is attached to the back of the cupboard door. My whole installation fit in unused space so took no storage room away from the RV.

I have to say I never thought I would have or like a central Vac in the RV but it works great and is so convenient. To follow are pictures of the installed unit.

05/18/2018

CEILING FANS

The bedroom in my RV has one window. On hot summer days there is not a breath of air in there and no cross ventilation. I thought how nice it would be to have a ceiling fan to keep the air moving at night.

About the time I was thinking about this some RV manufactures were beginning to install them but they used AC fans that ran either only when you had shore power connected or they ran them through a converter. These AC fans are large and heavy. I wanted to find a 12 volt DC fan that would run directly off the RV battery and had a remote control so that I did not have to run control wires. I found such a fan at http://www.rvstuff.com/ for $169.00 complete.

The next problem was installation. As most RVs have 12 volt power at every ceiling vent, including the air conditioner openings, finding power in the ceiling was not a problem. Routing could be however. I have found most RVs have rigid foam insulation in the ceiling or pink poly insulation. Routing through pink poly is fairly easy using an electrical snake. With a rigid foam ceiling I found a stiff electrical snake could push through the foam a fair distance without issue. When longer runs are necessary you can usually route to the air conditioning duct that then run the length of the RV then run the wiring through them.

To anchor the ceiling fan I took a page from the solar industry and used well nuts. They can hold almost anything to the thinnest materials. Well nuts can be found in the specialty section of the large box stores. Below is a graphic showing how they work.

To use well nuts you drill a hole large enough for the rubber of the nut to fit through. Insert the nut into the hole and with a bolt about ¼ inch longer than the rubber attach the bracket fan bracket to the ceiling. The well nut will compress in the hole holding the bracket secure.

Below is a nice graphic showing how well nuts work.

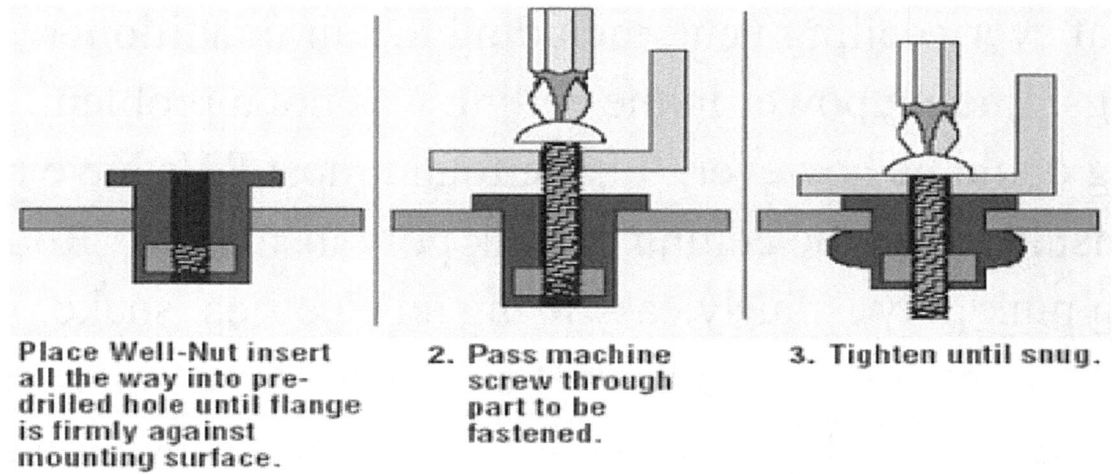

Having chosen a fan and solved the power and mounting problem it is time for the install.

When choosing the location to install the fan be sure it is clear of obstructions such as open cabinet doors and the slide walls when they are retracted. The picture shows the fan in the bedroom. As you can see it looks like it came with the RV.

This fan has been in my coach for eight years and has worked perfectly and never loosened despite 40,000 miles traveled. All the electronics are in the fan housing which is a plus. I have seen other 12 volt fans that require a junction box somewhere near them for the control electronics. This adds to the install complexity. Again the control is by IR remote the only connections are plus 12 volt and ground.

On occasion there will be a situation where the power wires cannot be routed in the ceiling. I ran into this situation in a tag axle coach. There I used conduit mounted to the ceiling with sticky tape to conceal the power wiring. I ran the conduit over to the air conditioning vent as we have discussed. Once in the vent I routed over to a ceiling vent and picked up power. Pictures of the install are above. Notice how good the conduit looks. It does not detract from the coach look at all.

This is where we picked up the 12 Volt supply at the ceiling fan vent.

The conduit was purchased from a big box store. It is self adhering and comes with all the pieces you will require. Price is $12.00 and is named "Mono-Systems, Inc. CordHider 9-Piece 144-in L White Raceway Kit"

Don't let that new door handle lock you in. Many of the handicapped door handles available for RVs extend out from the side wall when in use. When traveling they fold in against the RV. Are you aware that they can fold in over the entry door and trap one in their RV? This is a stunt young people like to play on old folks. To prevent being locked in you may wish to perform this slight modification.

Get a piece of 1/8" thick x 3/4" wide aluminum flat bar stock. This stock can be found at most any hardware store such as Lowes or Home Depot. Cut the stock to a length of about three inches or a size needed to block the handle. See the picture. Drilled two clearance holes using a 3/16" drill bit so two stainless steel #8 x 1/2" sheet metal screws can be inserted. With a 1/8" drill bit, drill two pilot holes in the plastic handle for the #8 screws. Hold the plate up to the handle to identify the location for the pilot holes. Attach the aluminum plate to the handle. You have now prevented the handle from folding over your door.

The nice thing about this modification is that it can be accomplished with the handle mounted on the camper. Aluminum and stainless steel screws are selected due to their resistance to rusting.

As you can see in the photo, when in place the aluminum stock completely prohibits the handle from being moved so it can lock in front of the door. The left folded travel position or fully open positions are not compromised.

Parts Needed:

1. 1/8″ thick x 3/4″ wide flat aluminum stock
2. Two #8 x 1/2″ long stainless steel screws

DOOR LOCKS, KEYLESS ENTRY

When I get to the campground I hate carrying my keys around. On top of this, shortly after purchasing my Berkshire I heard that the company uses only five different door keys for the entire fleet. Not believing this I went up to a buddy's Berkshire and for a lark tried my key. IT WORKED! Another upgrade/modification had just been born.

There are several excellent keyless entry systems available on the market that change out for the original RV door lock. Their prices normally begin at $300 and goes up after that. I looked into these products but not only was the price a discouragement, none were made to replace my style lock. Another solution was needed. I searched RV supply stores for months and finally in February found one that advertised a lock that would fit any RV door. Eureka! Not only was it keyless but it also had two key fobs. I ordered the lock and when it arrived put it on my pile of to do spring modifications.

Spring came and out to the motorhome I went with my new lock kit and various tools. I made meticulous measurements to the face of the door and door jam, drilled the necessary holes and began the install. It is then I found that the RV door was too thick and the drive bar of the lock would not reach through the door.   The lock was designed for a common 1 and ½ inch residential door and my motorhome door was two inches thick. Now what? I had a 2 and 1/8 inch hole in my motorhome door and no lock to fit and the wife saying "now you have done it".

Fortunately I had a buddy that owned a machine shop. I designed an inset filler plate that he fabricated for me. I painted the plate black, cut an even bigger hole in the interior of the door and mounted the plate. Fortunately everything worked out and the lock now fit.

You may notice that I mounted the lock upside down which allows me to access the dead bolt on the inside through the sliding door/window in the screen door.

Below are pictures of the installation. It looks great both inside and outside of the door. I have had this lock installed since 2012 and it has worked perfectly. The only maintenance I perform is to change the batteries every spring and it works great.

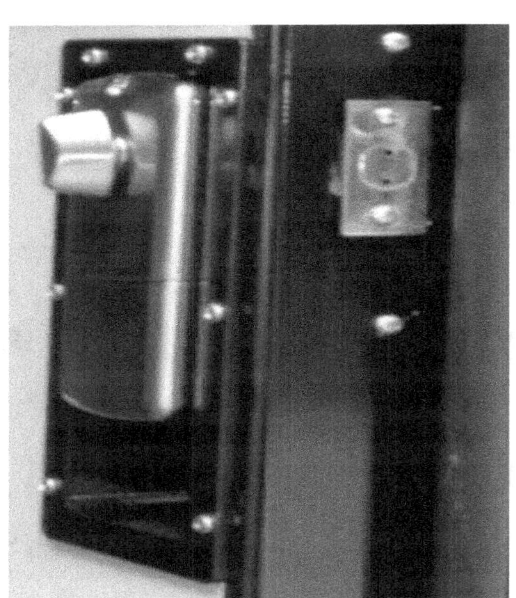 

Since this experience I have continued to research the use of resential door locks on RVs. I found that some manfacurers make locks specifically for thick doors like you find on fancy entry ways. These easly fit my thick motorhome door and eliminate the need for a insert plate. Some lock manufacturs like Schlage even make kits that will extend the drive bar to allow their standard locks to be modified into thick door locks.

Further on in this article are a couple of locks I have found designed for use on thick doors. They allow programming of a personal unlock code and can be purchased for less than $100.00. A special note when looking for an RV keyless entry lock I always look for one with a backup key feature and I now check all the dimensions to insure it will fit. The reason for the key backup is that most RVs have only one door. If the electric mechanism should fail the key gives you an alternative way to unlock the door. I hide a spare key outside the coach in a realestate lock box, an upgrade I discussed in my first book.

For installation I recommend a hole saw meant for cutting metal. While my door was fiberglass on the outside it had a metal core. This hole saw kit from Harbor Freight worked well for me and is very cost effective at $ 34.00

Harbor Freight 3/4 In - 2-1/2 In Bi-Metal Hole Saw Assorted Set 14 Pc.

https://www.harborfreight.com/34-in-2-12-in-bi-metal-hole-saw-assorted-set-14-pc-68990.html

As promised here are the locks I have found and used on friends coaches that accommodate thick doors.

"Schlage BE365VCAM716 Camelot Keypad Deadbolt. Designed to be used on doors 1 and 5/8 to 2 inches thick

https://www.amazon.com/dp/B000NJDRDA/ref=twister_B00NHQV1ZC?_encoding=UTF8&psc=1

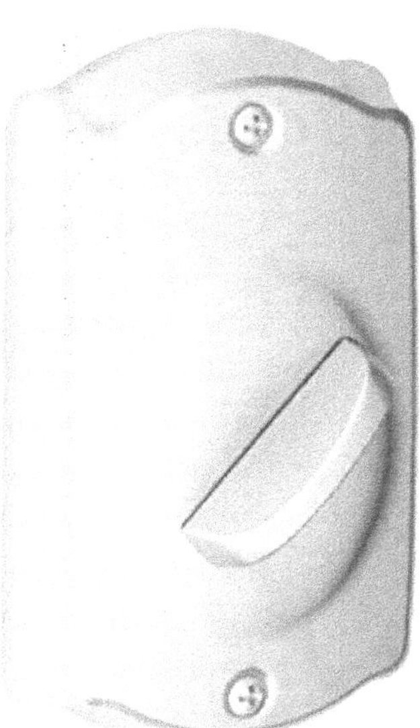

The following kits will allow the modification of a standard Schlage lock to a thick door lock. Price is about $24.00.

"Schlage Deadbolt Thick Door Pack BE365 Series | 1-7/8" - 2-1/2" Door Thickness"

https://www.doorlocksdirect.com/02-007.html

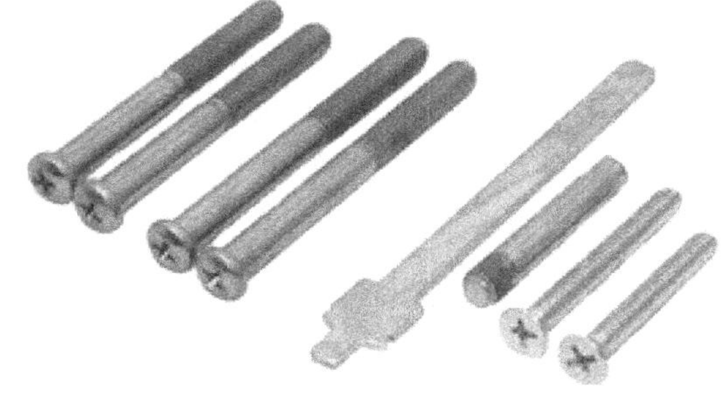

"BE469 / BE479 Series Deadbolt Thick Door Pack"

https://www.doorlocksdirect.com/23997877.html

If you are uncomfortable drilling into the door a locksmith can easily perform the installation.

FAN-TASTIC-VENT FAN REVERSE

During those nice hot sticky summer days known as the dog days of summer, wouldn't it be nice if you could cool the old RV a little more easily, or provide a breath of fresh air? Perhaps with this modification you can. I believe every RV has at least one ceiling vented fan and many have two or more. Most of these fans are set to exhaust the air. What if you could have one set to exhaust and one set to intake? This would create a nice air flow through the RV. Given these fans are nothing more than DC motors all you need to do to get them to run in reverse is to change the polarity of the power applied to the motor. This can easily be accomplished with a double pole double through switch wired as shown. The switch can be obtained from eBay. I have done this to two of my fans and it works great. All the information is provided.

2PCS 6Pin DPDT ON-OFF-ON 3 Position Snap Boat Rocker Switch AC 6A/250V 10A/125V

$0.99
Trending at $1.66
Buy It Now

From China

Top Rated
Plus

View of fan with new switch installed.

Detail wiring diagram.

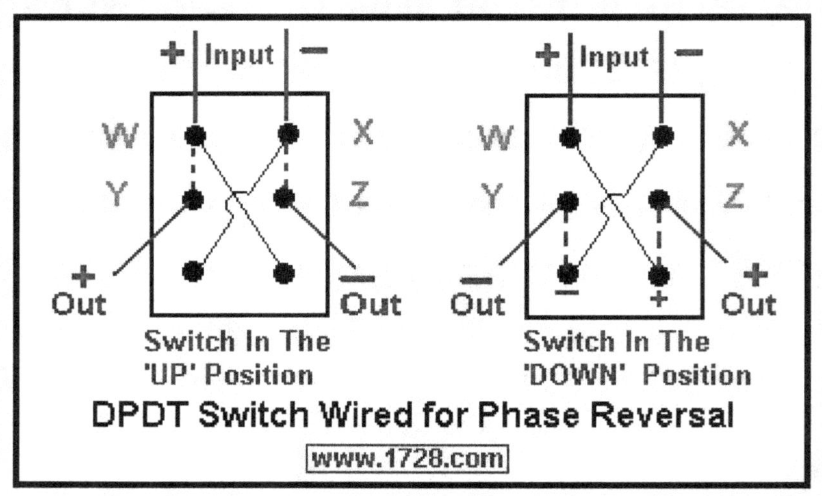

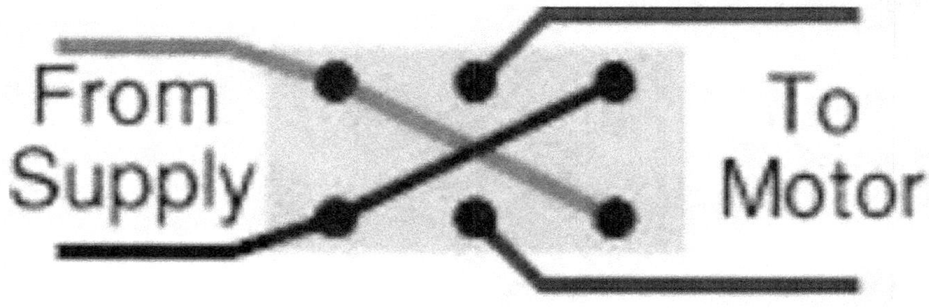

Do you have awning type windows that don't open very far restricting that fresh air flow on hot summer days? Looking at the hinge I know the window can open further but it does not. It appears that the only thing limiting the distance the window will open is the spacer in the window track. This spacer prevents the arms from moving closer together.

 To solve this problem opened the window just enough so that the track at the bottom of the glass, where the opener arms travel, will clear the side of the camper. Then removed one of the screws at the top on the hinge

outside and slid the window just enough so that one of the opener arms will come out of the track. Now remove the spacer then reinstalled the arm while sliding the window back into position. The result is a window that will open much further because the restriction has been removed.

When windows
are fully open
the arms being
too close
together causes
quite a bit of
flex. To solve
this cut down
the spacer to
about two
inches in

length and reinstall. Now the window will open further and the
mechanism still remains rigid.

The photo shows a double window. The left side has been
modified but not the right. See how much more the modified
window will open.

LED BULBS; WHICH ONE SHOULD I CHOOSE?

One of the easiest and most cost effective modifications you can do to your RV is to replace all the incandescent interior lights with LEDs. The advantage of LEDs is that they use much less power thus extending your battery life when boon docking. They will last tens of thousands of hours longer than incandescent. An LED bulb will probably never need to be replaced. They run cool so you will not get the heat buildup that incandescent lights cause making them safer. I have seen several melted incandescent light fixtures in my day. These could have caused a fire if not tended to. When changing out incandescent light fixtures, I have seen ever so many discolored ceilings caused by heat buildup. A very sobering sight.

In this topic I plan to discuss six bulb types. Those with a 921 base, those with an 1141 base, those that look like fuses, bulbs for the vanity and replacements for fluorescent bulbs. If you go to an RV show you can find any of these types of bulbs and will probably spend $15.00 or more for just one. You will be told how superior the bulb is and that it is specially designed to not cause TV interference.   If you ask me they are the same bulbs I get from China and the only thing special about them is the markup the seller is asking you to pay. My rule of thumb is to spend less than $1.00 per bulb, unless it is a special configuration. I have never had problems with longevity or TV interference with the bulbs I have purchased.

These are your 921 type bulbs. There are several LED replacements but I like this type. If you were to search eBay or Amazon you would be looking for "LED Bulbs 6000k Super White / 3500K Warm white 3020". You can easily find 20 of these for $15.00.

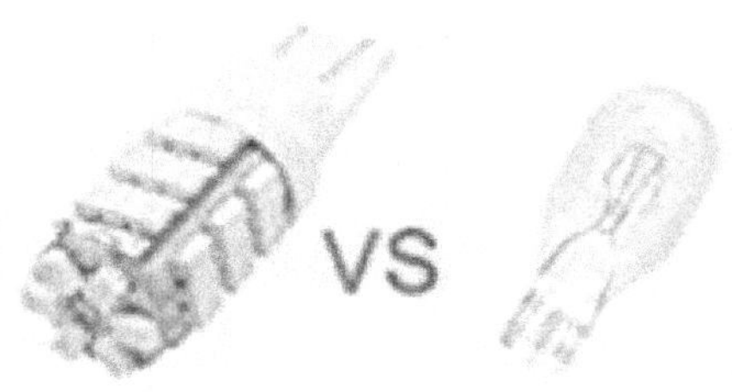

These are your 1141 type bulbs. I like the one depicted to the right. I have found these for as little as $13.00 for ten bubs and would search eBay or Amazon for "Warm White 1156 BA15S / 1141 / 1073 / 1095 Base 18 SMD 5050 LED Replacement Bulb For RV Camper SUV MPV Car Turn Tail Signal Brake Backup Light MA241"

This is a specialty type bulb used in the reading light shown. I had a devil of a time finding them but finally came upon one on eBay.

Search for "Indoor Vehicles 1156 Ba15s SMD LED Bulbs Lighting SUNSET WHITE in 280 LUMEN" I have found these for as little as $45.00 for ten and as much as $15.00 each.

This fuse type bulb is used in my step well lights and isle lighting. I found these on eBay by searching for "Dome License Plate Light Bulbs". Two bulbs set me back $3.00.

This is a vanity light replacement found at Camping World for $13.00. A little pricy but it is the cheapest I have found. We do not use the vanity much so I am waiting for this price to come down before I replace them.

The "600 Lumen White LED Replacement Panels for Fluorescent Lights, 2-Pack". Another Camping World find for $35.00. About the

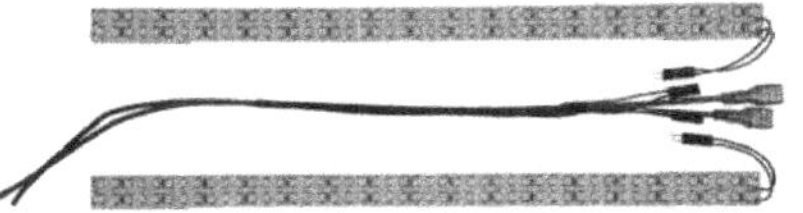

same price for two fluorescent bulbs but only change it once. This draws just 1 amp of current from your RV supply.

MEDICINE CABINET UPGRADE

I am constantly looking for a low cost solution to fix common RV problems. One that I have used often employs five gallon paint stir sticks. These are available at any of the large box stores for free. Just ask for them at the paint department. They are printed with the store name on one side but blank on the reverse side. I always keep a dozen on hand for quick fixes.

The first problem to be addressed is the RV medicine cabinet. We all have one and dutifully load it up with our tooth brush and tooth paste, aspirin, shampoo, and whatever. We drive to our campsite, have a great day, get ready for bed, open the medicine cabinet and out tumbles everything we have stored in there. Well a simple fix is to get a few Stir Sticks, Polly Stain to match the RV cabinet, some ½ inch number 6 screws, and a stubby screw driver. Stain the sticks to match the cabinet, cut to length, drill a hole in each end, and affix to the inside lip of the cabinet. They will act as a shelf guard. Problem solved. I have done this modification to many RVs and it works great.

FLASHING THIRD BRAKE LIGHT

You may remember this topic from my previous book but the option has been enhanced with flashing unit. This will make the third tail light even more noticeable to those following the coach. I went back to the 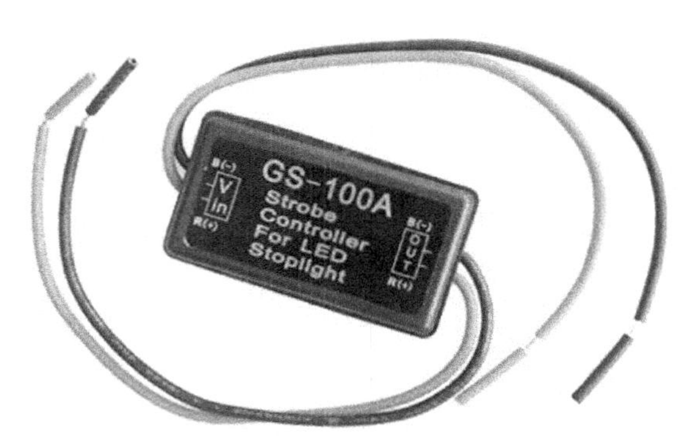 a point of connection which was behind the passenger side tail light. I took the wiring to the third tail light, cut the two connection wires and spliced in this simple flashing unit. Now when the brake pedal is pressed the third tail light will flash three times quickly, three times slowly, and then stay on solid until the brake pedal is released. This new option cost only $7.00 and I found it on Amazon here:

https://www.amazon.com/Podoy-GS-100A-Controller-Flasher-12V-24V/dp/B01F4OKWSG/ref=sr_1_2_sspa?ie=UTF8&qid=1530899717&sr=8-2-spons&keywords=brake+light+flasher&psc=1

The flasher unit and third tail light are wired as follows. A very simple modification and great safety feature.

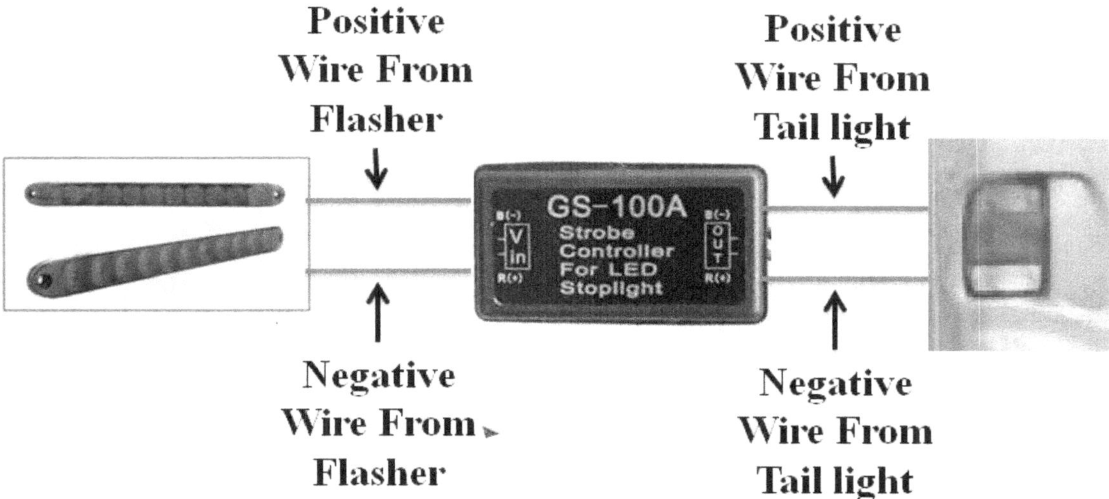

Original third tail light

A few years ago on my way home from an international RV rally I had an opportunity to follow several different motorhomes. One thing that stood out on these coaches was how noticeable the third tail light on the back was. I began to think that this was a real safety feature and I should have one. On my return home I went to Amazon and found this for $23.00 CCIYU 15" Waterproof Red Sealed 11 LED Light Bar Truck Trailer RV Stop Turn Tail 3rd Brake Light (Pack of 2 pcs).

The back cap of my motorhome is hollow which made them easy to install.

I drilled one ½ inch hole for each light to route the wires then just screwed the lights on. Once mounted I simply removed the tail light on each side of the coach reached in and connected the third tail light to the coach lights.

I found the lights here:

https://www.amazon.com/ECCPP-Waterproof-Sealed-Light-Trailer/dp/B01IP7J8PC/ref=sr_1_3?ie=UTF8&qid=1531016240&sr=8-3&keywords=Waterproof+Red+Sealed+11+LED+Light+Bar+Truck+Trailer+RV+Stop+Turn+Tail+3rd+Brake+Light

Cramped for space in the kitchen? Check this out, the HomCom Portable Rolling Tile Top Drop-Leaf Kitchen Trolley Cart. Folded it measures just 16.25w x 14.75D x 29.75H in. Unfold the wings and get a 36 inch island. Comes complete with a

drawer, vegetable baskets, and comes on wheels so may be easily rolled in a corner when not required. A great way to expand the kitchen prep space or even use as a small table and cost is just $50.00.

You can find it here:

https://www.amazon.com/dp/B00FW75YYS/ref=asc_df_B00FW75YYS5294386/?tag=hyprod-20&creative=395009&creativeASIN=B00FW75YYS&linkCode=df0&hvadid=167124260587&hvpos=1o4&hvnetw=g&hvrand=15577352222735991254&hvpone&hvptwo&hvqmt&hvdev=c&hvdvcmdl&hvlocint&hvlocphy=9001885&hvtargid=pla-304609628564

PROGRAMMABLE THERMOSTAT OUTLET

Cool new gadget time! I use electric radiant heaters to supplement my propane furnace in the RV when it is cold. They are more cost efficient in the long run as I pay for the electric in my campground fee.   It also becomes a pain when the propane gets low and I have to fire up the motorhome to get more. One area you travel trailers and fifth wheels benefit over motorhomes is portable propane bottles, but this article is not about my wonderful heaters. It's about a totally amazing outlet adapter, the Lux WIN100 Heating & Cooling Programmable Outlet Thermostat

The only real issue with many smaller space heaters is that they either do not have thermostats, or the ones they have are highly inaccurate. The the Lux WIN100 Heating &

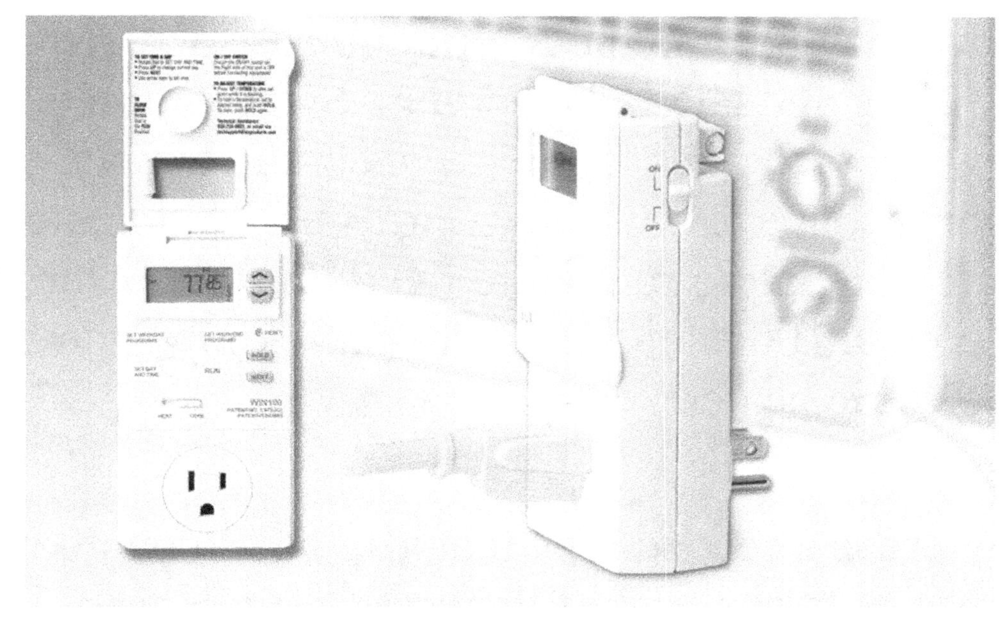

Cooling Programmable Outlet Thermostat will not only turn your heater on and off, but will also turn a fan on and off or an electric room air conditioner if you use one.

It can be programmed to be different on weekends! Come on, now... That is pretty damn handy for a price tag under $35.00. You can find this little guy here

https://www.amazon.com/Lux-Heating-Cooling-Programmable-Thermostat/dp/B000E7NYY8/ref=redir_mobile_desktop?_encoding=UTF8&dpID=61pVmJLNSrS&dpPl=1&psc=1&refRID=PF0T4M3K6WHXPNM4RTAB&ref_=pd_aw_sim_201_2

Another use for this gadget is to control a heat source in your wet bay to keep the RV plumbing from freezing during early spring and late fall camping. Set it to turn your heat source on when the temps fall below a certain temperature and turn the heat source off when it warms up. Automate the process of you having to run out to the RV to check the heat. I myself use couple 100 watt light bulbs but I know many people use little electric heaters.

Here is a second type that also has a countdown timer function, useful for control of lighting or appliances.

Houzetek
MO
CURRENT
CD/
RND/
+
SET/
MODE
ON/
OFF
RESET

PIN SWITCHES

Many of us have lights in the compartments of our RVs but for one reason or another never use them. Often the light is in an inconvenient location or the slide out is over the compartment and one would need the arms of a gorilla to reach the light switch to turn it on. A solution I have found to this problem is to install pin switches on the door frame. These switches will turn the light on automatically when the door is opend or closed. The way this works is that the light is left on. The pin switch is connected to the negative side of the light wiring. Whenever the door is open the switch will connect the wire and complete the circuit turning the light on. The light wiring can be accessed by taking the light down from its mounting location. Snip the ground and add wire to run it to the location you choose for the pin switch then reinstall the light.

When choosing which of the two wires going to the light to route to the switch I choose the ground or negative side. The negative side is attached to the pin switch as often the switch will be connected to the chassis frame by its mounting method. In this case if you attached the positive it would result in a short and blown fuse.

There are two style doors often found on an RV. One has a frame as shown above. For this style of door I recommend the switch below.

https://www.amazon.com/Pactrade-Marine-Security-Adjustable-Switch/dp/B01JASKG24/ref=sr_1_39?ie=UTF8&qid=1492048403&sr=8-39&keywords=pin+switch

The second style door has a flush frame. As depicted in the picture below.

For this style door I recommend the following switch be used

https://www.amazon.com/Nickel-Plated-Switch-Polycarb-Plunger/dp/B001TQWOOO/ref=pd_sim_107_5?_encoding=UTF8&pd_rd_i=B001TQWOOO&pd_rd_r=FHZPZA32DCVABBME3KM0&pd_rd_w=biuWk&pd_rd_wg=kwmrE&psc=1&refRID=FHZPZA32DCVABBME3KM0

Do you travel with your feline friend? If yes where do you keep the litter box? An RV is so small that where ever you choose it will probably be in the way. Here I will present two ideas for a cat litter box that will be easy to take care of and also be out of sight and out of mind.

The first is the **Ottoman**/coffee table litter box.   The **Ottoman** can be purchased from Amazon for about $35.00. Also purchase a cat door for about $10.00. Install the cat door in the end of the **Ottoman**, line the inside of the **Ottoman** with some type of plastic like a shower curtain and place a litter box on the opposite side as the door is installed. Install a motion sensitive battery LED puck light, place the top on and you have a litter box that nicely stores in front of the RV sofa and can be used as a foot rest and or coffee table.

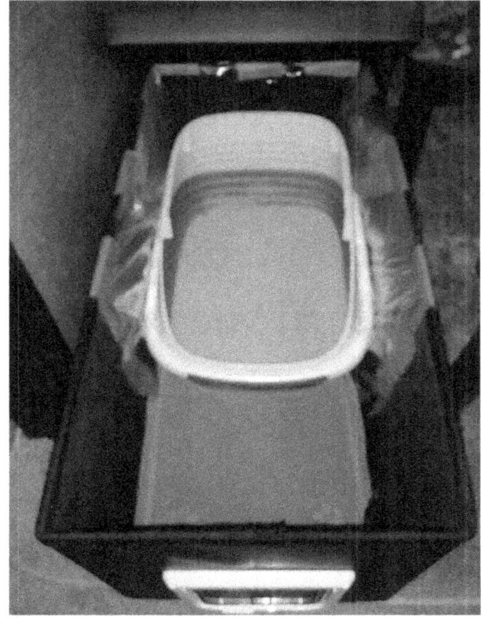

The Ottoman and cat door can be found at these addresses:

https://www.amazon.com/Otto-Ben-Folding-Storage-Ottoman/dp/B010U5M4P8/ref=sr_1_2_sspa?ie=UTF8&qid=1518956990&sr=8-2-spons&keywords=ottoman&psc=1

https://www.amazon.com/PetSafe-Interior-2-Way-Locking-White/dp/B00061RIT4/ref=sr_1_4?s=pet-supplies&ie=UTF8&qid=1518957620&sr=1-4&keywords=cat+door

Perhaps you do not have room for an Ottoman. Another idea is to do the same thing but put it under one of the dinette seats. The same cat door can be installed in the end  of the seat. Again line with plastic and place the cat box and motion sensitive LED light under the seat. Cleaning is done from the top as most dinette seats have access to their storage from under the cushion. A facsimile can be seen above.

My mother used to say "do not let your wants hurt you". Well for the last several years I have wanted a recliner in my motorhome but the original furniture still sits and looks new as is evident in the picture to

the right. Last fall while browsing through eBay RV stores I came across the RecPro store.

http://stores.ebay.com/Recreation-Pro?_trksid=p2047675.l2563

Among other things they sell RV furniture and there staring at me was a twin recliner love seat. Heeding my mother's advice, I am no longer wanting a recliner for the motorhome. In other words I purchased the

loveseat recliner. Due to lighting when the two pictures were taken the fabric color looks different but in reality they are almost identical.

To remove the jack knife sofa from the motorhome I first removed the seat and then the back. Each was held on by four bolts and it only took a couple of minutes. I then unbolted the frame from the floor. This was held down with carriage bolts that went through the floor of the slide. I was surprised that each section of the sofa weighted no more than 25 pounds and easily fit through the RV door.

The new love seat came in four sections, the two seats and two backs which made loading into the motorhome easy. I assembled them in place, ran six lag screws  through the front frame (being careful not to go through the slide floor) and using two of the lag screws from the original love seat and a homemade bracket, I bolted the back of the love seat in place. I left room at the side next to the wall for storage of a wooden side table. The wife was pleased so I would call the installation a success.

Have you ever
experienced one project
spawning another? That
is what happened here.
Behind the love seat was
a large space just perfect
for out of sight, out of
mind storage. The
problem, how to get to
the things stored back
there. The solution, a
custom box made to

slide behind the love seat. The box can be pulled out to access
items placed back in the corner. To protect the love seat and
wall of the coach I attached pipe foam to the sides of the box.

Now you might be thinking that is a nice upgrade but I cannot
afford a reclining love seat that nice or perhaps the space where
I would install new furniture is a different size or configuration.

Let's address the cost first. I found my zero wall clearance
reclining love seat on sale for only $600.00. Believe me if it
were into the thousands like many I have seen it would not
have happen. Just because the price was low that does not
mean the quality was low. The love seat is well made and so
comfortable. After our first season camping with it installed

the only problem I have had is getting to sit in it as everyone else does.

Now to configuration, RecPro has many styles and sizes, and fabric choices of chairs, love seats, and sofas to choose from. I know that there would be one to fit your needs. If not you can configure a custom solution from their easily assembled parts. That is actually how my love seat was made. Remember I said that it came in four sections. Below I show just some of the sections you can choose from to build your custom solution.

There are of course left and right sides.

A number of center sections have different features like cup holders and storage.

They have many types of individual chairs in different configurations and fabrics.

They even have a chair that can turn into an ottoman with storage and for only $99.00. How cool.

Now you may be thinking this section has turned into an advertisement for RecPro. It was not meant to. I am just so pleased with their product and price point I wanted to show just a small sampling of what they offer for RVs.

The time has come. You look at the old RV and it is beginning to look a little long in the tooth or the wife says "I am sick of this entire wood decor" wouldn't it be nice to paint everything white? I say white because as I write this article that seems to be the popular color. I don't plan to get into color choice but white in something that will be used

in the wild outdoors? Not my choice but whatever floats your boat. So off to the hardware you go, Buy one of those products that has prime and paint in one and is guaranteed to cover in one coat and you attack the RV. It looks beautiful then time passes. Six or ten weeks pass and that fresh painted wall looks like the one above.

It seems nothing will stick to the common RV wall. This is because the material the wall is made from is a man made product that is covered with a contact paper like product. This product is almost a vinyl like material with some type of slippery finish. So what now? As I see it you have two choices. First, find a small child and have him or her go at the wall. As we all know children can mark anything! Second, is proper preparation of the surface to be painted. If done correctly the preparation will actually take longer than the panting but the results will be worth the effort.

First, if you made the mistake shown in the picture, all that paint you have applied needs to come off.   I am sorry but there is no way around it as the paint will continue to peel no matter what you apply to it. Once you have the walls back to the way they were when you started then you can begin anew.

First step is to remove anything that is attached to the wall. This will include switch plates, wall socket covers, hooks, and pictures. Now wash down the wall to remove all dirt and grease that has accumulated over the years. I like to use warm water with a little Dawn dish soap and wash rag. Be careful around electric wall outlets. To be safe you can unplug the RV from the pedestal. When it comes to cleaning I actually do my whole RV, walls and ceiling every spring. You will be surprised how dirty the wash water will get. For my forty foot RV I need to change the water three times.

Once washed you now need to scuff the surface with a fine grit
sand paper.   I would do this by hand as you do not want to
remove the top coat material, just scuff it up so that there is
more surface for the paint to grip to.

Wipe the newly sanded walls with a tack cloth and perform
another cleaning with the warm water and Dawn. Let the walls
dry thoroughly. If in summer, this will happen fairly quickly
because as we all know most RVs are hot boxes.

Once dry go around edges you plan to paint with painters tape.
I use to do my painting free hand but learned over the years
that painters tape really does save time and makes for a neater
job.

Now you are ready to prime the
walls but do not use just any
prime. The best prime for the job
is Glidden Gripper. From what I
have read and from my own
experiences this is the magic
sauce that makes the previous
steps work. Other products may
claim to work but after all that
hard work you have already performed I would use a proven
product.

Once the Gripper is dry
choose your desired color
and paint. You should get
the same type of results as
shown. A beautiful
smooth coverage that will
last a long time.

REMOTE LIGHT SWITCH

This is something for shall we say the height challenged among us. How many have ceiling lights and or ceiling fans in their RVs and no wall switches by which to turn them on? So many manufacturers use the switches on the device which is on the ceiling and the only way to reach them is ether have a tall spouse turn things on or use a stool. Another solution, install a remote control device.

The first one I want to discuss is strictly for LED lighting applications. Not only will it allow the remote turn on/off of the light but it also provides for dimming of the light. The main module is the size of a pack of cigarettes and can be mounted next to the light or in the ceiling above the light. Simply

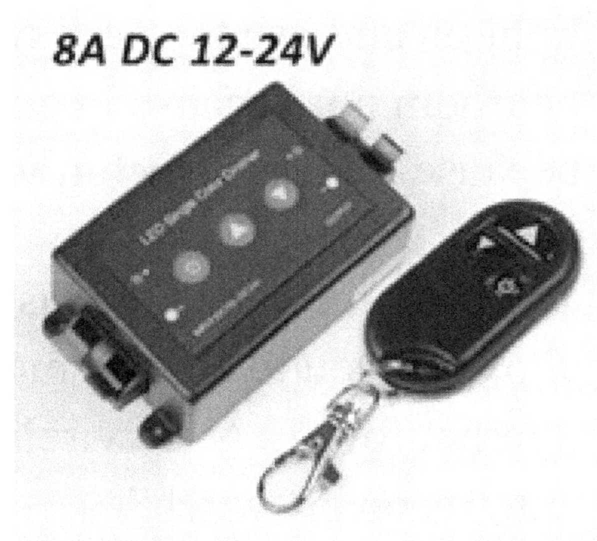

cut the wires to the light and attach them to the control module input then the device to be controlled to the control module output. The installation is complete. The remote control is the size of a key fob.

This device may be obtained at the provided web address. I
have installed this and it works great.

http://www.banggood.com/8A-DC12-24V-LED-Strip-Light-
Single-Color-Dimmer-Controller-With-Wireless-R emote-p-
987970.html

Here is a real nice remote switch that a friend brought to my
attention. Like the other it is installed in the hot line of the
light, may be hidden behind the light, then you simply leave the
light on and use the new switch. I may put these in the
bedroom not because I cannot reach the light switch but
because I cannot reach it while in bed.

The switch can be purchased with from one to three receivers
allowing you to control multiple lights. If interested search the
internet for "12 Volt wireless on off remote control transmitter
with receiver switch"

The maximum price I have seen for this item is $35.00 for the
three switch set.

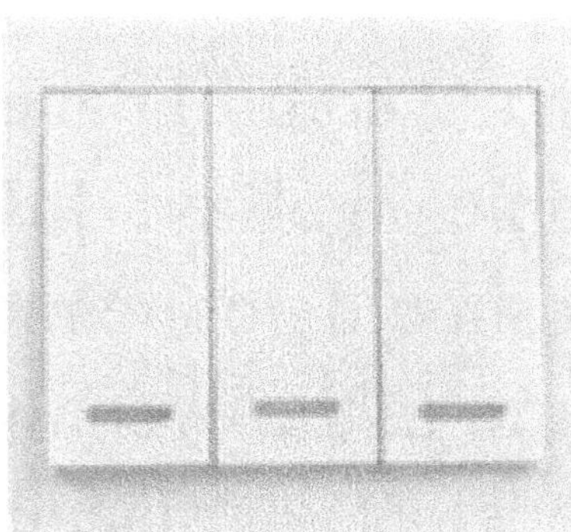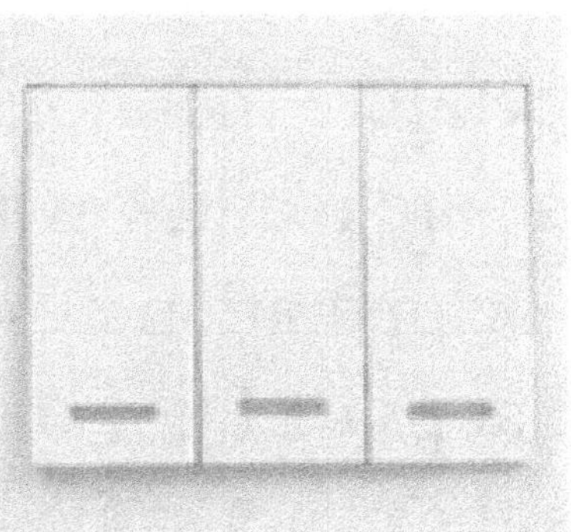

REFRIGERATOR TEMPERATURE MONITORS

How many of you know how well your RV refrigerator is cooling? I would imagine not too many. Even if you have a thermometer in the refrigerator by the time you open the door and retrieve it, it will have warmed by some amount thus providing an inaccurate reading.

I read about this modification on an RV forum, liked it and have done it about ½ dozen times. Mount 12 volt digital temperature monitors in the control panel of the refrigerator. These are readily available on eBay. Just be sure to look for 12 volt dc operation. Cost should not be more than $4.00 each. At that price I got an extra in the event of a failure I would have the exact same model as a replacement. The thermal couple wire is run down the hinge side of the frame. I held mine in place with a dab of GE silicone, then ran the temperature bulbs, one into the freezer compartment and the other into the refrigerator, and secured them with tie wraps to a shelf.

The front panel of the refrigerator is removed by depressing two clips, one on each side. You have to look to see them. Using a multi meter you can test connections on the refrigerator control board to find 12 volt power that is on when refrigerator is on and off when refrigerator is off.

After

REFRIGERATOR TEMPERATURE MONITORS (REV II)

For those of you that are not handy, there are several products that allow you to monitor the temperature in both your refrigerator and freezer. Installation is a breeze. You just need to replace the batteries every year. Cost is from $15.00 to $25.00 depending which one you choose.

The product name is "AcuRite 00986A2 Refrigerator Freezer Wireless Digital Thermometer"

https://www.amazon.com/AcuRite-00986A2-Refrigerator-Wireless-Thermometer/dp/B004QJVU78/ref=sr_1_3?ie=UTF8&qid=1509236957&sr=8-3&keywords=Refrigerator+Digital+Thermometer

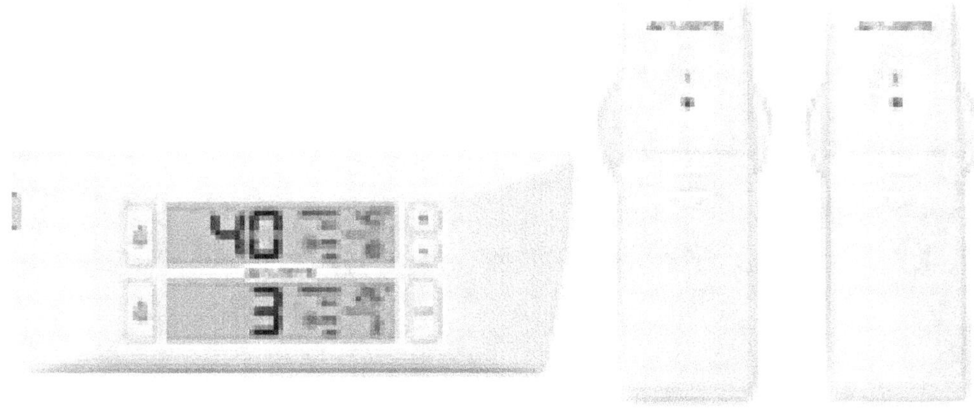

Another product is "Refrigerator Thermometer Wireless Indoor/Outdoor Digital Sensor with Audible Alarm"

https://www.amazon.com/gp/product/B076Q6XKVW/ref=s9_a csd_zwish_hd_bw_bjv039_c_x_w?pf_rd_m=ATVPDKIKX0D ER&pf_rd_s=merchandised-search-8&pf_rd_r=2PPNHRXGEBVA9R4NQMZC&pf_rd_r=2PPNH RXGEBVA9R4NQMZC&pf_rd_t=101&pf_rd_p=86836e7e-7851-5b79-855a-83c4312eaba8&pf_rd_p=86836e7e-7851-5b79-855a-83c4312eaba8&pf_rd_i=678520011

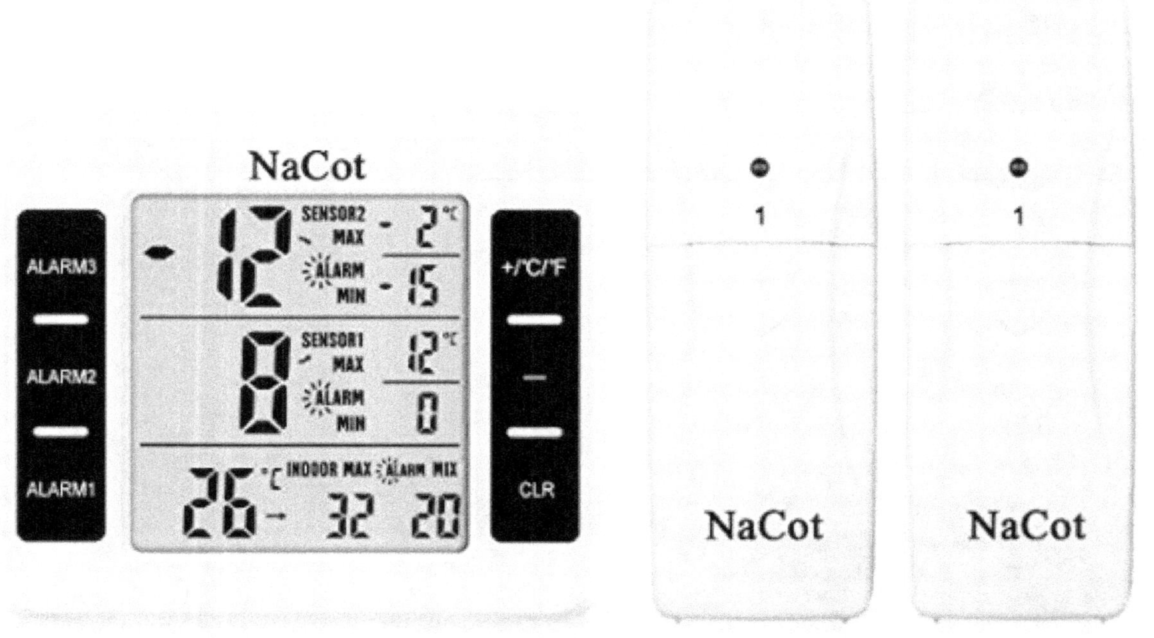

The final product that friends have recommended is" 【NEW VERSION】 Indoor Outdoor Thermometer, Refrigerator Thermometer, Sensor Temperature Monitor with Audible Alarm Temperature Gauge for Freezer Kitchen Home"

https://www.amazon.com/VERSION%E3%80%91Indoor-Thermometer-Refrigerator-Temperature-Included/dp/B07F8N2H98/ref=lp_678520011_1_24?s=kitchen&ie=UTF8&qid=1544324412&sr=1-24

REFRIGERATOR COOLING IMPROVEMENT

I have often read that an RV refrigerator will run more efficiently if you can exhaust the heat from the back of the unit. There are many kits on the market that claim to do this for you at the cost of $65.00 for a basic kit to over $100.00 that runs the fan off a solar cell. You can however make one of these kits yourself for a few dollars.

I did this by purchasing a thermal switch on eBay that closes at 45 degrees C. The switch was $4.00 for two. I then went out to the net and found two quiet 60db fans. Because of their size they would not fit in the refrigerator stack. My solution was to fabricate a directional duct for one and have the other blow directly onto the exposed condenser.

Thermal Switch, Normally Open, 45 Degree C

Tap for 12 V Power

This worked so well I was able to get the same cooling and turn my refrigerator settings down by half.

Below are the pictures of the duct and install. The duct is cardboard wrapped in aluminum tape.

REFRIGERATOR AND CUPBOARD DOOR LOCK

Today most of your high end motorhomes and fifthwheel RVs come with residential refrigerators. The problem with these 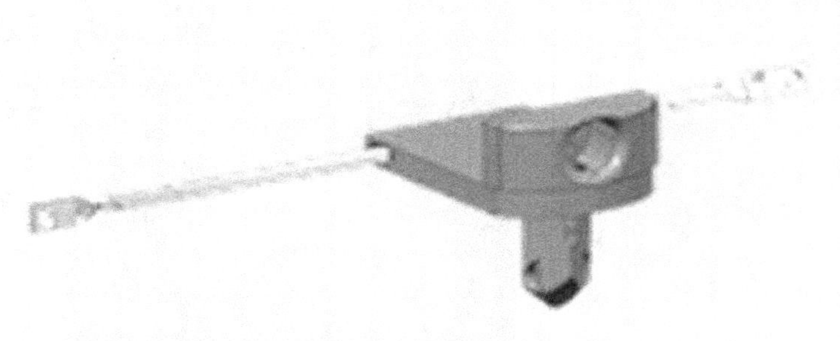 units is holding the doors closed while traveling. Many people try to use bungee cords or some other device inserted into the door handles but these do not really work well. Recently I came across a product called the Frig Fixer. This neat little product not only holds the doors closed but can be used to prop the doors open when not in use and the product is magnetic so when you arrive at your destination it is stored on the face of the refrigerator. The web site for this product is:

https://www.recubed.solutions/

Cost varies depending on the type and model refrigerator you have and can be installed in minutes with no modification to the refrigerator. Below are pictures of the Frig Fixer with doors locked and unlocked and in their storage position. It is in the unlocked position that the magnets come in handy.

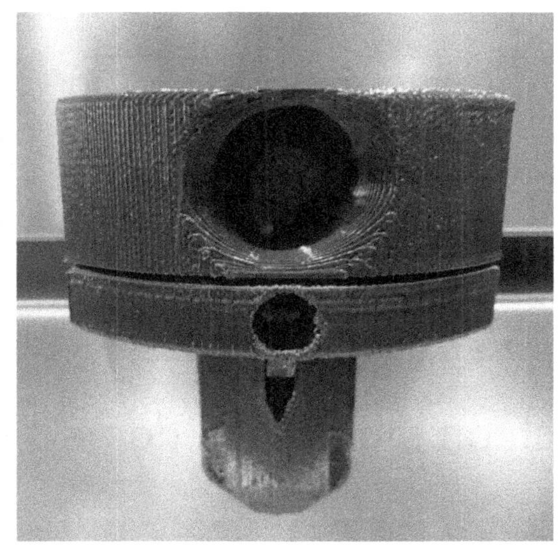

Here is another lock I have heard some coach manufactures use. This one would be less visible and cost is under $30.00.

"Sugatsune, Lamp HC-85/S Catches and Latches, 304 Stainless Steel, Brass, Satin"

If you have a interest check out this web page.

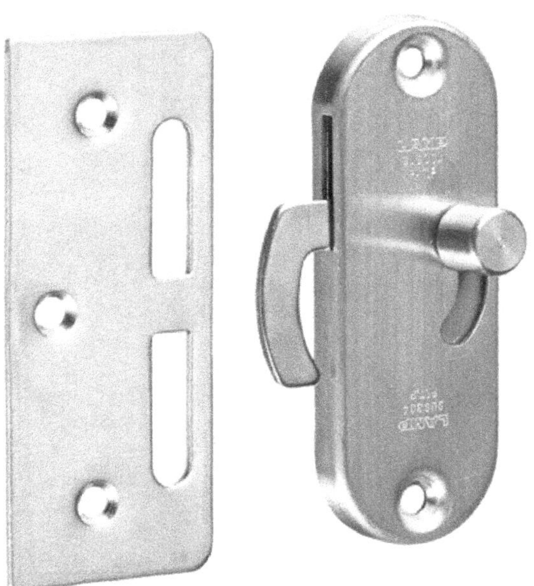

In the pictures below you can see this latch on the French doors of a residential refrigerator.

This is the latch fixed to the freezer sliding draw. Notice how the striker plate is attached to the wall next to the refrigerator.

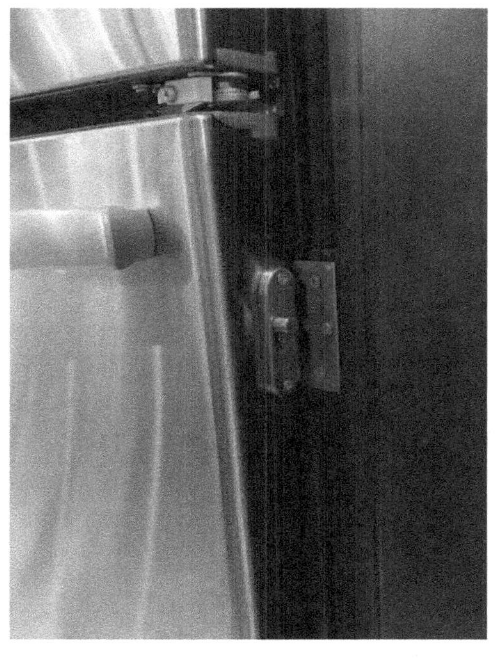 

Then there is this solution that will only cost you your time. It is a U shaped wedge to put between the door handles. I have made several of these to keep cupboards from opening. I find old plastic election signs are the perfect material. It holds up great and will not scratch what you are sliding it on to. You can always dress the lock with some craft ribbon. A lot of people use this method.

Here are the cupboard locks I mentioned. These I made from the plastic lids of coffee cans. I did this after hearing stories of cupboards opening behind the side walls of slides, not being noticed, and great  damage happening when the slides were opened. I felt better safe than sorry. All my cupboards behind slides now have these. They are easy to install and take off and store just inside the cupboard door.

Twelve years ago when I was shopping for my first motorhome leveling jacks were optional and I had to check the motorhome's configuration to ensure they were included. Fast forward to 2018 and leveling jacks are standard on all Class A coaches, many Class C motorhomes, and one can often find them on fifth wheel and travel trailers. We have come a long way but along with this progress comes another chore to be performed while setting up camp and more accessories to be stowed in the RV and carried from place to place. What am I speaking of? Jack Pads. Those wonderful items made of wood, plastic, or rubber that you put down on the ground for your jacks to rest on. Now you might say why use pads at all. I just let my jacks rest on whatever surface is under the RV whether dirt, stone, concrete, or asphalt. That thought is great until you camp where jack pads are mandatory or you deploy your jacks on an uneven surface and bend the foot. Now you have a repair that will cost several hundreds of dollars.

If your RV is like my motorhome the jacks are well inboard and the motorhome is close to the ground. To position jack pads I need to crawl on my belly. This is a PIA and I have often thought there must be a better way. Well last year I found it. A product called SnapPads. SnapPads are jack pads made from recycled automobile tires that install once then remain on the jack's foot forever. No more carrying extra pads or crawling under the RV when setting up or breaking down. Simply arrive at camp and push the auto level button and you are done.

My motorhome has an Equalizer leveling system with ten inch round feet so I required the SnapPad EQ product. They arrived two days after I ordered them and installed in just 30 minutes.

As I mentioned previously SnapPads are made from recycled automobile tires. The product is well made and when holding them they feel substantial and durable. While I did not weigh them I would estimate the pads I purchased to be maybe eight pounds. They are two inches thick and twelve inches in diameter. The pads are designed with a lip and groove for the jack foot to snap into. There is a hole in the center to allow for jack maintenance (ie. to get to the jack pad attachment bolt if required) and slots in the side to ensure water will not be trapped in the pad. To follow are some photos I took showing off the SnapPads' features.

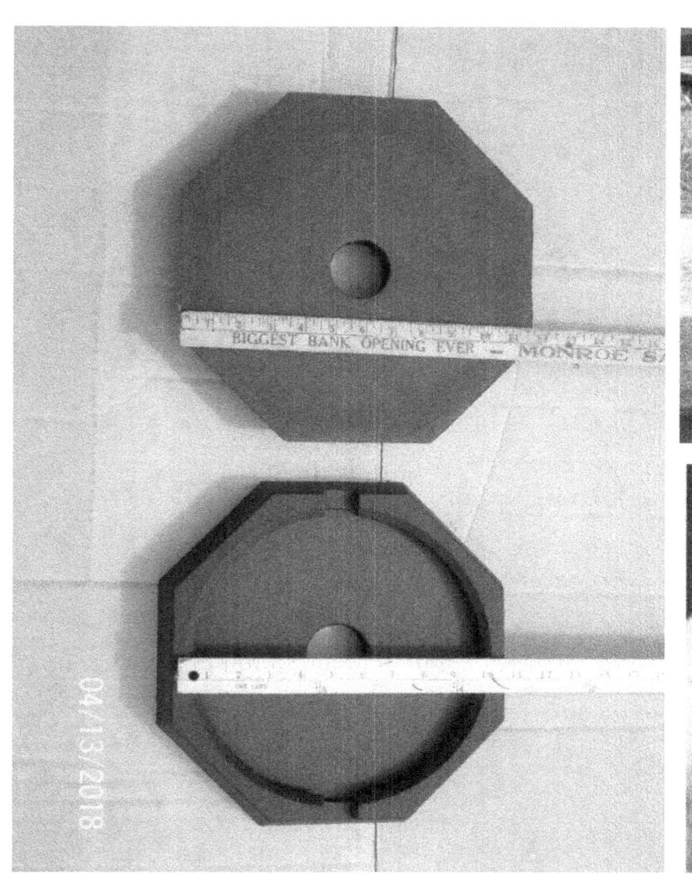

Installation was literally a snap. As recommended in the instructions I placed a liberal amount of dish washing soap around the rim of the pad. I then centered the pad under the jack and communicating with my wife using our cell phones I had her deploy the jack. As the jack lowered onto the pad there was a distinct snapping noise signaling installation was complete. It could not be any easier. To follow are pictures of one of the SnapPads installed on my coach.

SnapPad Benefits are:

- Permanent jack pad & leveler
- Adds unparalleled stability
- Easy one-time installation
- Rubber dampens vibrations
- Anti-Slip - excels on all surfaces
- Water drainage channel helps remove excess water
- Environmentally friendly - made from recycled tires
- Protects against electrical surges (lightning strikes)
- Protect your driveway from rust marks
- Two-year warranty

The company currently has four styles of SnapPads that fit the most popular jack systems. These are

SnapPad Xtra: Made for LCI's Level up & Ground Control 3.0 & TT Leveling Systems with 9" round landing feet.

SnapPad PRIME: Designed for us with 10-inch round Power Gear & Kwikee 'Level Best' leveling systems* for Class-A & Class C motorhomes.

SnapPad HiWay: Two designs for HWH leveling jacks:
HiWay 8 for 8" round landing feet.
HiWay 10 for 10" round landing feet.
HiWay Plus for Tiffin's with 8" front and 10" rear landing feet.

SnapPad EQ: Two designs for Equalizer leveling jacks:
SnapPad EQ Octagon for 10" OCTAGONAL landing feet.
SnapPad EQ Round for 10" ROUND landing feet.
SnapPad EQ Plus for motorhomes with 2x round front and 2x octagonal rear landing feet.

The SnapPad web site may be found at https://rvsnappad.com.

SMART TILE KITCHEN BACKSPLASH

This is by far one of my favorite modifications. You get a big bang for short money and time. Having an older coach the backsplash in the kitchen area was finished with just wallpaper. For some time I have wanted to dress this up. A couple of years ago I read an article on Smart Tiles. Smart Tiles are a vinyl product that comes in 10 inch by 10 inch sheets, has the appearance of tile, and has an epoxy backing. I have continued to follow this product and read where others have had great success applying it in their RV's. Some have followed up on their success one and two years after application and confirmed the product still looks like new. I decided to give it a shot.

While Smart Tile is a brand name for the product which can be purchased through stores like Amazon, Lowes, and Home Depot there are other brands that come up if you do a Smart Tile search. I chose to go with Tic-Tac-Tiles because they had the pattern and color scheme I preferred.

Preparation involved removal of any loose paper on the backsplash and then a through cleaning with a degreasing agent. Tools needed for the work were a razor knife, scissors, straight edge, cutting board, and measure. From collecting the tools to applying the tiles and clean up only took three hours. I finished the edges with ½ inch chair rail stained maple to match the coach.   I was so pleased with the results I even did the backsplash of the two vanities.

Unless you actually touch the product you cannot tell it is not real tile and even then they can fool you. They are anti mold/mildew treated, water proof, and only added ten pounds to the weight of the coach. See the included pictures of before, during, and the completed job.

In Process. Loose Paper removed and wall pre cleaned

Tiles can be cut with Knife or Scissors

Completed

Before Center Vanity

Completed Center Vanity

Completed Bath Room Vanity

SOLAR

I researched this project for over a year reading hundreds of white papers and talking to even more people. One thing that became apparent back in 2016 was there were a lot of companies installing solar on RVs but none were documenting the why or the how.   Starting from nothing and after my year long research I felt ready to begin specifying my system.

I decided I wanted monocrystalline type solar panels, an MPPT charge controller and I needed a minimum of 175 watts of solar to sustain my energy needs. Energy use is going to be different for everyone. I took into consideration that my wife and I were very thrifty with our RV energy. I have a generator if I needed to run the coffee pot, microwave, or air conditioner. All I needed the solar for was to replenish the batteries after a day's use of the ceiling fan, lights, cell phone charger, power used by the gas refrigerator controller, propane detector, and TV. I also wanted a system that could be expanded if required.

Through my research I decided I would purchase the bulk of the needed material from Renogy Solar. Armed with my requirements I began to design my system. As I did the costs kept climbing and climbing until I realized it would be cheaper to just purchase one of their 200 watt package deals. The problem with the 200 watt package was it was maxed out and could not be expanded, so I settled on the Renogy 300 watt MPPT package. The timing was near Christmas 2015 and Renogy had their packages on sale. By waiting until Cyber Monday I was able to secure an additional 15% discount over the sale price. After purchasing switches and mounting hardware my total installation cost was $733.51.   Really not bad. Here is a breakdown of the material:

KIT-PREMIUM300D-MT Renogy 300 Watt 12 Volt Monocrystalline Solar Premium Kit	$623.23
15 FEET SunGen Solar Panel Extension Cable Wire (15 Ft.) with MC4 Connectors	$9.99
6 FEET UL Solar Panel Extension Cable Wire (6 ft) with MC4 Connectors	$11.99
Marine Knob Battery Master Isolator Cut Off Power Kill Switch Control 12/24V	$18.08
Winegard CE-2000 RV Roof Cable Entry Plate	$8.56
12V-24V DC Auto Car Bike Stereo Audio Circuit Breaker Reset Fuse Inverter GBNG 40 Amp	$8.25
100X Nylon Cable Zip Tie Mounts 20*20mm Self-Adhesive Wall Holder Mount Clip DIY	$2.98
Solar panel mounting hardware from www.mcmaster.com	$50.43
Total	$733.51

We dry camp about two weeks each year. I have used this system several times and after an evening with lights and TV going and two ceiling fans running all night, my batteries have been fully charged no later than 10:00 each morning.

Before we continue let's talk about solar terms you may encounter.

Solar panels

As you enter into the solar world you will encounter two types of solar panels, polycrystalline and monocrystalline. Both will do the job but there is a difference. The silicon used to manufacture the polycrystalline solar panels is of lower purity so they are not quite as efficient as monocrystalline solar panels. For this reason I choose monocrystalline panels for my install. By sight it is very easy to tell the difference between the two types. Polycrystalline cells are square in shape while monocrystalline cells have their corners cut off. You can see this in the following pictures.

Monocrystalline

Polycrystalline

Solar Controllers

Next there are solar controllers. Again there are two types or technologies used PWM (Pulse Width Modulation) and MTTP (Maximum Power Point Tracking). In simple terms PWM controllers take the voltage from the solar panel to charge the battery bank. If the solar panel produces 18 volts as many 1 watt panels do and the batteries need 14 volts to charge the PWM controller will throw away 4 volts. MPPT controllers on the other hand convert this excess voltage to current and use it to charge the batteries. This is a more efficient use of the power being delivered by the panels. There are other differences but this is the biggest. You can easily tell the difference between PWM and MTTP controllers as true MTTP require transformers to do the voltage to current conversion which make them much bigger in size. I chose to go with a MTTP controller for my installation.

Battery Bank

A battery bank is necessary to store the power created during the day for use at night. The battery bank should always be made up of deep cycle batteries. For our RVs they will be configured as 12 volt banks. This is accomplished by connecting batteries in parallel, or series, or sometimes both. When constructing a battery bank the important thing to remember is battery voltage in series will add together while the current will remain the same. The opposite is true for parallel combinations. Currents will add and the voltage will remain the same.

Say what!!!???

Don't worry as I have an example. Let's say we are building our battery bank using six volt 200 amp golf cart batteries. If we have only two they will be connected in series and we will have a battery bank value of 12 volts at 200 amps.

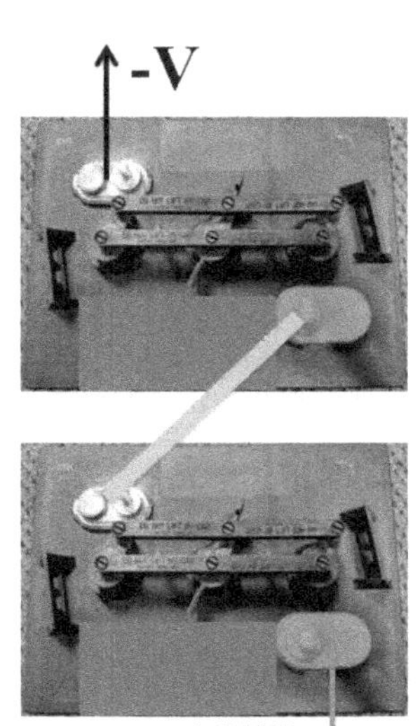

Now let's say we are building our battery bank using four, six volt 200 amp golf cart batteries. We would first make two series banks like the one above then connect those two banks in parallel. The result will be a 12 volt 400 amp battery

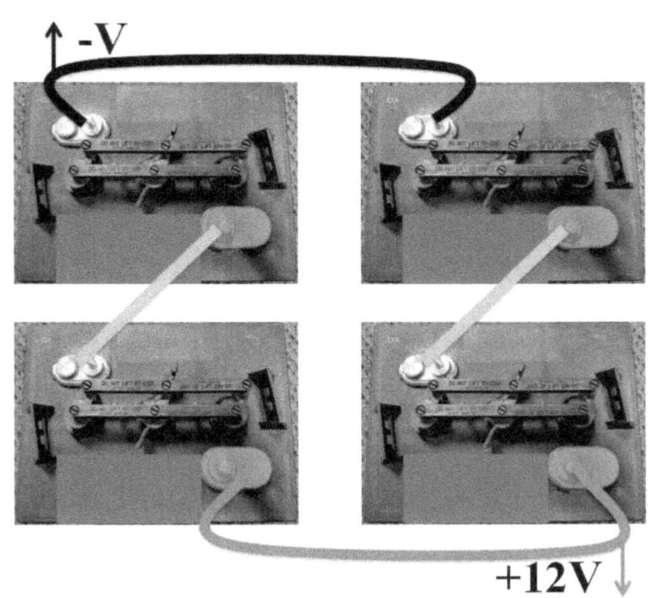

bank. This is the size most common in solar installations.
Notice when using a four battery bank it is best to connect
your cables at the corners as I have shown. This will allow
the batteries to stay balanced.

MC4

The connector
style used on
solar panels and
solar cables.

Solar Array

This will be one or more solar panels configured into a
group and integrated into a system. Whether the panels are
configured in series or parallel will often depend on the
type of controller in use.

If the controller is PWM panels are normally connected in
parallel. Remember PWM controllers discard any energy
greater than that needed to charge a battery. For that
reason they are about 85% efficient.

If the controller is MTTP the configuration is normally
series or a combination of series and parallel. In the
transmission of electricity the higher the voltage the more
efficient the transmission is. In addition MTTP controllers

use all the energy created. This is why they are considered 99% efficient. Both of these are reasons to build series combinations of panels.

Inverter

An inverter is necessary if you wish to change the 12 volt battery power to 120 volts AC, the type of power found in a residential home. This is required to power appliances and entertainment devices. The  best type of inverter to purchase is a true sin wave inverter. At least a 2000 amp is necessary to power anything of size.

Inverter Charger

This does just what its name implies. It is an inverter like the one described above but also has a battery charger in the same package. When connected to the power 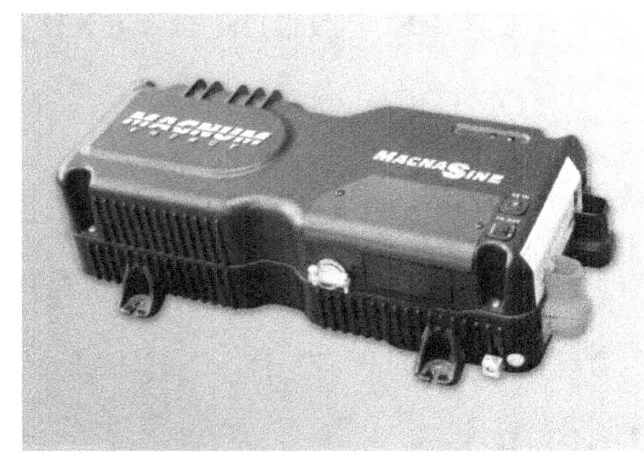 pedestal it will charge the batteries along with the solar system. Most of my experience with these devices is with the brand Magnum Energies. They make various sizes.

Wire Gauge

Finally we get to wire gauge. This is a very important topic because too small a gauge connecting your system will starve the components of power. Think of wire gauge like a water hose, the larger the diameter hose the more water comes out. The same is true of wire. The heavier the wire the more power it can conduct.   The only catch is that the smaller the gauge numbers the thicker the wire. Now doesn't that make sense? I went with 10 WAG to connect the solar panels and 8AWG to connect to the battery bank. Watch this specification as some kits use smaller gauge wires. I only needed 175 watts of solar to do the job I wanted but went with a 300 watt kit to get the larger wire gauge. The 300 watt kit was still cheaper than configuring a 200 watt kit with my specifications. I looked at it as getting an extra 100 watts of solar. Extra capacity for me.

What does a typical solar system look like? You basically take all the parts I described above along with a few others and configure them into a system. I have included a basic system diagram.

Basic solar design,

Red wire is positive, black is negative.

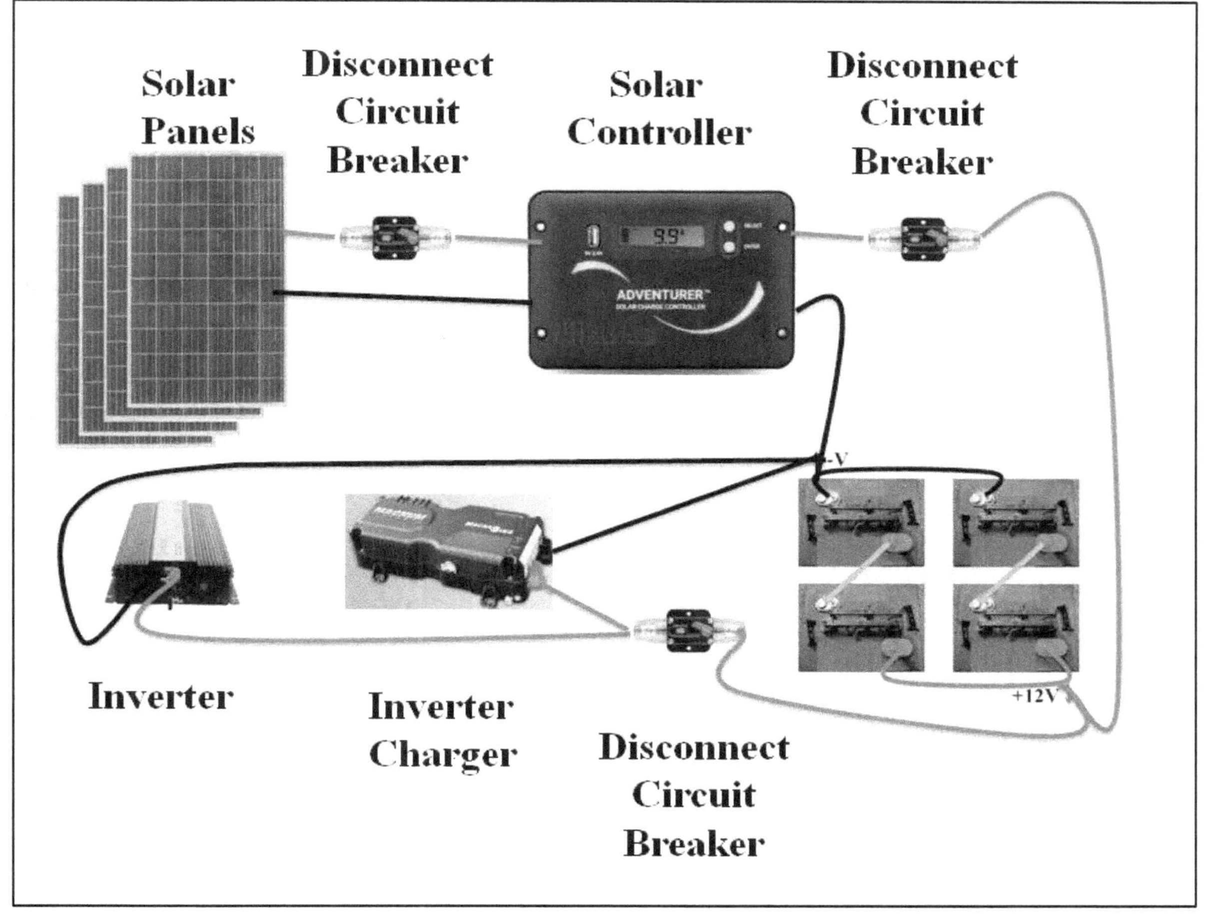

Back when I installed my solar I chose to go with a Renogy kit and I still like them. The kits have become even better now containing everything you might need. If doing another install I would choose among their premium kits. Two that I like are their 200 watt kit with MTTP controller and 300 watt kit with MPPT controller. Both are expandable and the controller can even be programmed through Bluetooth from your phone.

These kits can be found here:

https://www.renogy.com/renogy-new-200-watt-12-volt-solar-premium-kit/

https://www.renogy.com/renogy-new-300-watt-12-volt-solar-premium-kit/

They have kits all the way up to 1200 watts if you feel you need more capability. At the end of the article I have listed other popular solar companies. You cannot go wrong using any of them.

Solar panel install:

There are a lot of discussions on this topic. Two popular are; should they be on tilted brackets and how do you fasten them.

First the bracket:

I decided since I had excess capacity in my design I would install the panels flat on the roof of the RV. I had no interest in climbing up there to tilt the panels.

Now the fastening question:

You will not believe how many people will not drill holes in their roof but instead ues to tape, Velcro, or only dicor to attach their panels.   I just want to say I do not want to follow these people down the road. I have seen panels blow off and a flying panel is not easy to dodge. The solar panel must be anchored and anchored well. Renogy recommends the use of their Z brackets and well nuts to anchor their panels.

Well nuts can hold almost anything to the thinnest of materials. Well nuts can be found in the specialty section of the large box stores. 

Below is a graphic showing how they work.

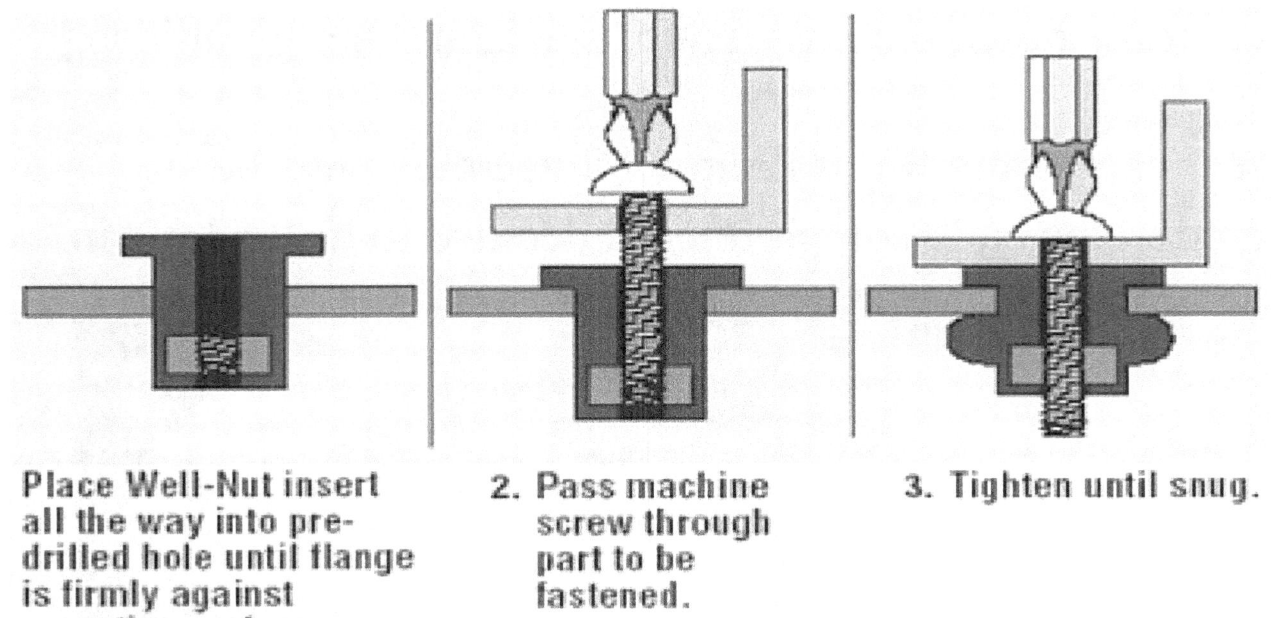

Upon securing the panels I followed up with an ample application of dicor around the brackets and screw heads to prevent leaks. My panels have been installed for two years. So far no leaks and solid as a rock.

To get the maximum from my solar panels I wired them in series. The panel wiring is held down to the RV roof with dabs of dicor.

Now the question of routing the wires from the roof to the RV basement and to the solar controller. There are several ways to accomplish this. Some people will drill holes in their gray water tank vent stack, route the wires down the stack, then seal the holes. This is a great idea.

 Others route down the refrigerator stack, another great idea.

The rear cap on my RV is hollow. Since the controller is mounted in the back compartment I decided to drill a hole in the top of the cap, route the wires down the hole, and seal the hole with a cable routing plate and dicor.

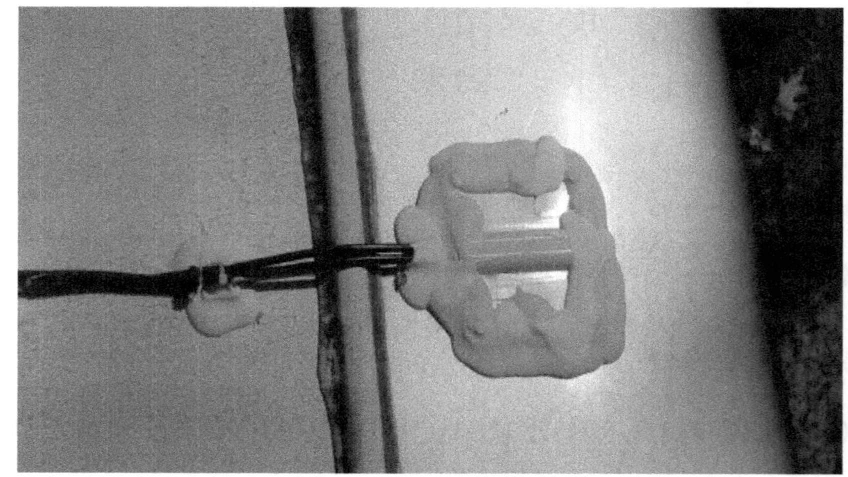

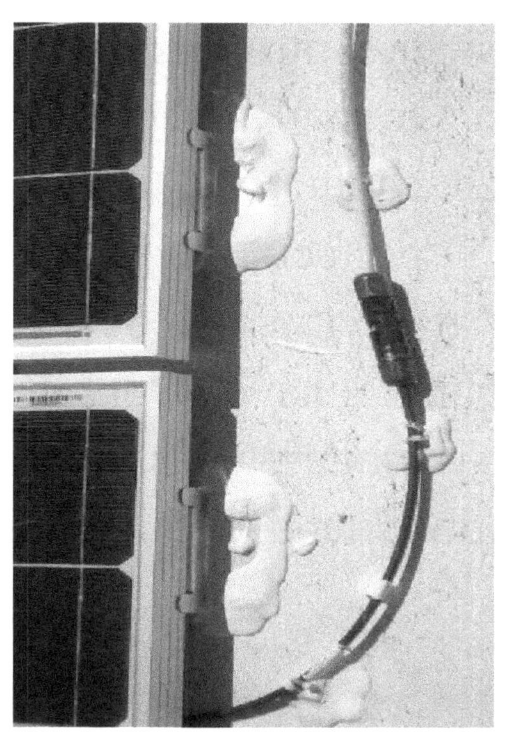

Everything you read says to install the solar controller near the batteries so as to minimize cable length. On my RV the inverter/converter is in the back basement cabinet and the batteries are in the cabinet right next to it, perfect. I mounted the solar controller using two wooden slats so it would be away from the wall allowing air flow and cooling. I have an on off switch and fuse between the controller and solar panels. I have another resettable fuse between the controller and the batteries.

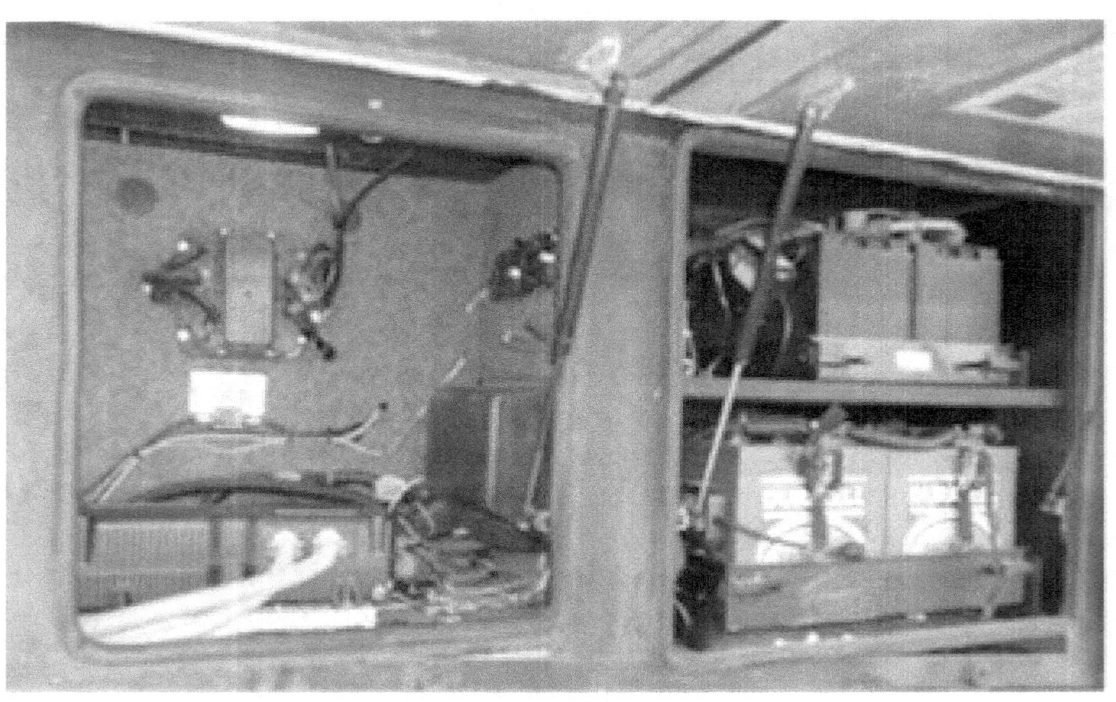

Photo Showing Location of Electronics Bay With Respect to Battery Bay

Renogy MPPT 40
Amp Controller
Photo Panel
Disconnect Switch
04/14/2016

40 Amp Fuse and Battery
Disconnect Switch
04/14/2016

One topic that I could find absolutely no information on was if you need any special considerations when installing a solar controller on an RV that has an inverter/converter. Would the two fight each other when charging the batteries? The answer is no. If the Renogy solar controller sees elevated voltage on the battery bank from another charger it will shut down.

The MTTP controller I selected is capable of talking to a remote information and control panel. The last portion of my install was to route a CAT4 cable into the cabin of the RV and connect this control panel.

Some web sites that I found useful in my information search are listed below

http://gpelectric.com/products/solar-flex-kits-modules

https://www.windynation.com/

https://www.renogy.com/

http://samlexsolar.com/

How many of you have that six to eight inch space next to the shower or the bath vanity? I know that I do and about the only thing it is good for is collecting dirt. Here an imaginative RVer turned that space into a towel cubby. I applaud their imagination.

Over the years I have seen accessories that I thought made organizing and storing travel trailer towing equipment easier. I decided it was time to group these together into one article.

Let's start with the safety chains. These come pre attached to the tong of the travel trailer and are often too long. How many times have you seen a camper pull into the RV park with his chains dragging? After a couple hundred miles of this the RV owner will be in the market for new 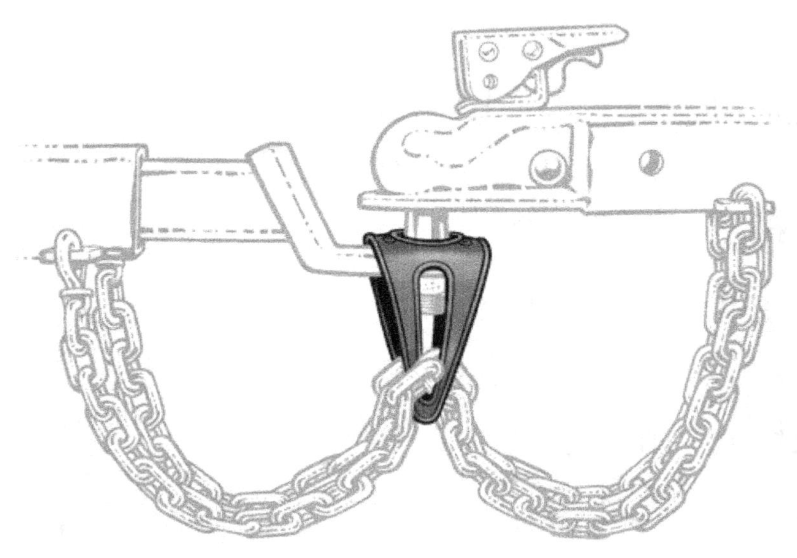 chains. As a solution to this problem you can cut the chain to a more proper length or maybe remember to twist them prior to connecting to your tow vehicle in effect making them shorter but not as flexible in turns. There is another solution I have seen, Chain-up Safety Chain Holder. This slick device is only about $8.00 and cradles the safety chains so they will not drag.

This neat device can be found on Amazon here:

https://www.amazon.com/Equal-i-zer-82003065-Chain-Up-Mount-Hitch/dp/B00HJ6YN6A/ref=sr_1_3?ie=UTF8&qid=1523407530&sr=8-3&keywords=chain-up

Once you arrive at the RV park and unhook you now have to stow your tow equipment. I often see the safety chains, brake away switch wire and trailer electrical plug left to lie on the ground. Along with them getting dirty and messy to handle it is not good for the electrical plug. A slick solution to this issue is a Tongue Jack Trailer Towing

Organizer. The organizer connects to the jack post of the trailer. It costs about $20.00, and provides a cap to keep the connections in the electrical plug clean and a location to store everything.

This neat device can be found on Amazon here:

https://www.amazon.com/Tongue-Trailer-Towing-Organizer-Plastic/dp/B01F9ILPTM/ref=sr_1_2?s=automotive&ie=UTF8&qid=1523408359&sr=1-2&keywords=Towing+Organizer+%7C+Chain+Saver+with+Plug+Saver

The last items that need to be taken care of are the ball hitch and torsion bars, if you use them. Now these are rather expensive and you do not want them to walk away. I have seen  two slick ideas to both secure and store these items. While a bit pricy at $150.00 this item attaches to the A frame of the travel trailer and provides a location to lock down the torsion bars and hitch head saving valuable space in your RF storage cabinets.

It is named EzStorHitch and can be found here:

https://www.amazon.com/EzStorHitch-Securely-Distribution-Reclaim-Storage/dp/B01FMFN3FQ/ref=sr_1_1?ie=UTF8&qid=1523455970&sr=8-1&keywords=ezstorhitch

An alternative to the EzStorHitch is to mount a two inch receiver to the tong of the RV. The ball head can be locked to this receiver. Then mount two PVC pipes ether in a cabinet as shown in the picture or under the frame of the RV to slide the torsion bars into. Simple and easy.

UNDER CABINET DRAWERS

A under cabinet drawer is a good way to use that open space under any cabinet hether in the kitchen, living area or bedroom. To follow are some I have put in associates' RVs in the past and they have worked out great.

The "ANYThing Keeper - Office Desk Organize - Kitchen Storage & Cabinet Organizer, RV space saver" comes in black or white with a cost of about $30.00.

https://www.amazon.com/ANYThing-Keeper-Organize-Kitchen-

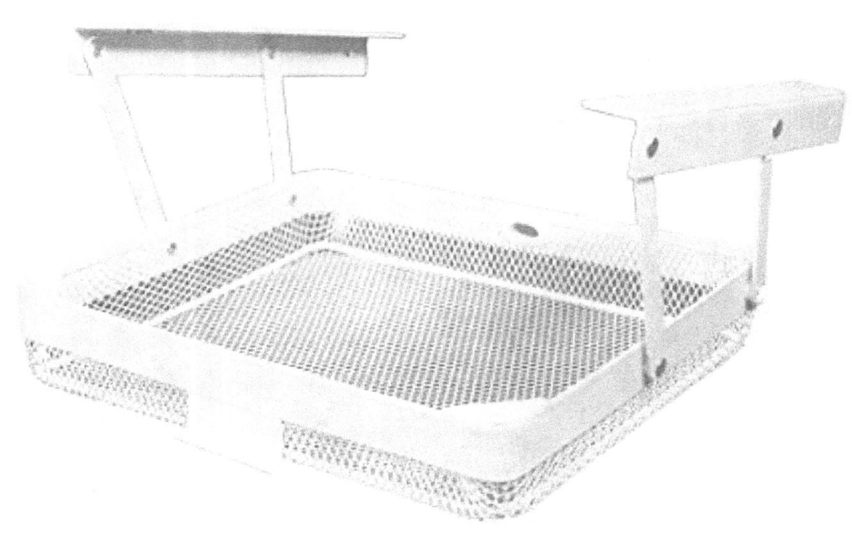

Organizer/dp/B07D8JYV73/ref=sr_1_1?ie=UTF8&qid=15297 90521&sr=8-1&keywords=anything+keeper

The "Coffee Keepers Under Cabinet K-Cup Holder". Sells for about $19.00 and can be found here:

https://www.amazon.com/Coffee-Keepers-Cabinet-Holder-608938498274/dp/B005F0JM7W/ref=sr_1_2?ie=UTF8&qid=1529790521&sr=8-2&keywords=anything+keeper

The "Rubbermaid Pantry Organization Under Shelf Pull Out Drawer, Small". Sells for $12.50 and can be found here:

https://www.amazon.com/Rubbermaid-Pantry-Organization-Under-Drawer/dp/B004P1IH46/ref=sr_1_3?ie=UTF8&qid=152979052521&sr=8-3&keywords=anything+keeper

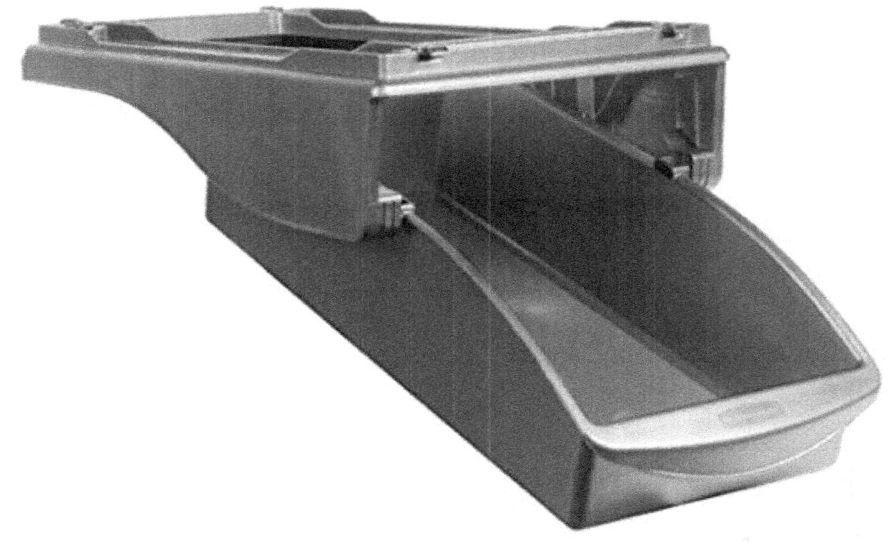

The "Rubbermaid Slide-Out Under-Shelf Storage Basket, Titanium (FG1H3200TITNM)". This useful item can be used inside a cupboard under the shelf or under the cabinet for a fruit basket. Sells for $23.00 and can be found here:

https://www.amazon.com/Rubbermaid-Pantry-Organization-Under-Drawer/dp/B0018DV796/ref=sr_1_3?ie=UTF8&qid=1529790521&sr=8-3&keywords=anything%2Bkeeper&th=1

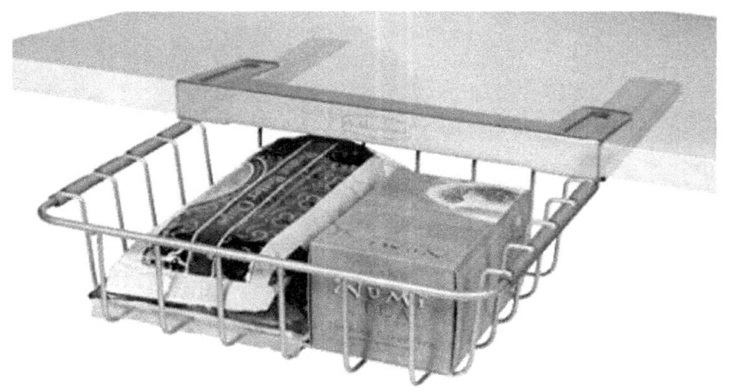

"Under Cabinet Sliding and Folding Kitchen Storage Organizer". Find it on Amazon for $23.00/ Web address is:

https://www.amazon.com/Cabinet-Sliding-Folding-Kitchen-Organizer/dp/B00DP5R1WW/ref=sr_1_4?ie=UTF8&qid=1529790521&sr=8-4&keywords=anything+keeper#customerReviews

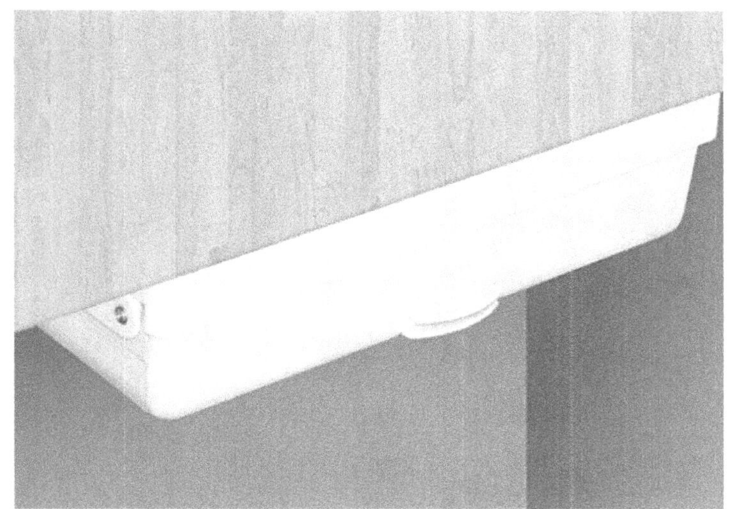 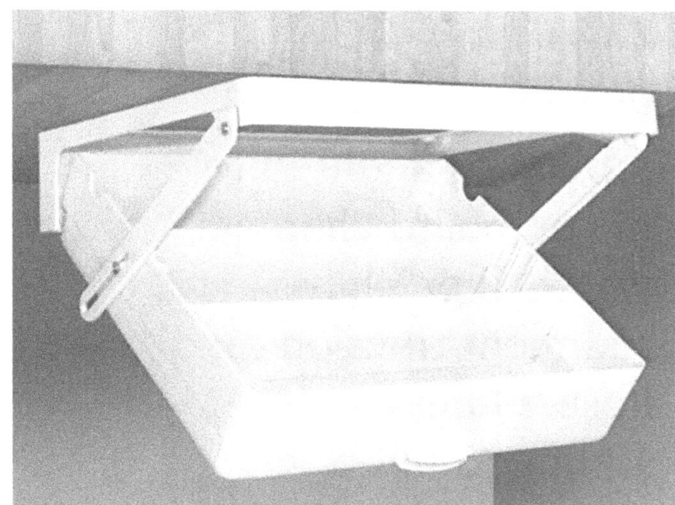

WATER SOFTENER

Let's talk water today. Many of my friends are tired of the water quality found in campgrounds. Most often you are getting untreated well water through 50 year old piping. In addition to the on board charcoal water filter I have a sediment filter on my hose. Others are adding to this a portable water

softener. I asked one friend and he has The Go OTG4-Std Soft RV Water Softener.

On the go Standard Softener-features easy to carry handle, large mouth opening for easy salt addition, quick and easy regeneration, easy and fast hook-up and its compact space-saver design results in much lighter weight

The softener provides soft water that prevents hard water & rust stains, avoids scale build-up, improves taste and odor, increases lifespan of appliances and will also improve rough dry skin while increasing lathering of soaps.

Built for the owner of any RV/Marine model, this 8,000 grain unit is a perfect fit. It simply regenerates with 1 box of common table salt in less than 15 minutes and provides the owner with soft water up to 20 days.

It's compact size allows it to be installed in the tightest places. It will allow high flow rates with very low pressure drop.

It utilizes a standard garden hose connection between park faucet and your RV, requires NO tools or electricity and its compact design 22" h X 6.75" dia. can be easily stored in your storage bay or dock side locker.

I found it here for a great price:

https://www.rvupgradestore.com/RV-Water-Softener-p/standardsoftener.htm?gclid=EAIaIQobChMIirH4ptyc2AIV27bACh1qTAD2EAQYBSABEgITL_D_BwE&gdffi=d722fab84a06472899ce2a16e4d2ed3f&gdfms=6CCAD7EB970D4F16A05621BBE0CAB02D

WATER HEATER UPGRADES

In this article I would like to take the opportunity to discuss a couple of upgrades that can be done to your tanked RV water heater. The first will be an electrical conversion and the second the addition of an adjustable thermostat.

Many tanked water heaters today have both electric and gas heating elements. The RV owner may choose one or both to provide hot water to their camper. Older RVs and what may be referred to as entry level RVs often just have gas heating elements. Several years ago an owner of one of these RVs asked me if there was any way he could convert the water heater to electric. I had read about such conversions but had never done one or known anyone with one. I told my friend it could be done but I did not know how well it would work. We proceeded with the conversion and I am please to say it far surpassed our expectations.

The product I used was a "Camco Hot Water Hybrid Heat Kit" that cost roughly $80.00. These kits come for both six gallon water heaters and ten gallon water heaters. This install was on a six gallon tank but since then I have also installed one on a ten gallon tank with the same great success.

Providing you don't mind the on/off switch being by the hot water tank, everything you need to do the install is in the kit. Follow the easy to read instructions and you cannot go wrong. The kit is designed to be plugged into a 120 volt AC socket so if one is not available you may need to have it installed.

Now I said providing you don't mind the on/off switch being near the tank and you have a nearby electrical receptacle everything you need is in the kit. My friend however, wanted the switch to be located on his master panel and of course there was no electrical receptacle. I ended up tying into a nearby junction box which solved the electrical problem and a spool of wire and a little work chasing it to the control panel solved the switch problem.

I need to emphasize if you are not comfortable with electricity have an expert do that portion of the job. For added safety have the RV unplugged from the electrical pedestal until the install is complete. Only then plug the RV in and check your work.

Here is what was involved to complete the install.

The water heater was turned off and checked to be sure tank was cool. The drain plug or in some cases anode rod was removed from the tank as

this is where the heating element is installed. The heating element was installed using Teflon tape around the threads.   A hole was drilled in the side of the water heater mounting flange close to the gas line. The wires from the heating element were then run into the RV.

Inside the RV a section of the Styrofoam was cut away from the hot water tank to allow the mounting of the thermostat.

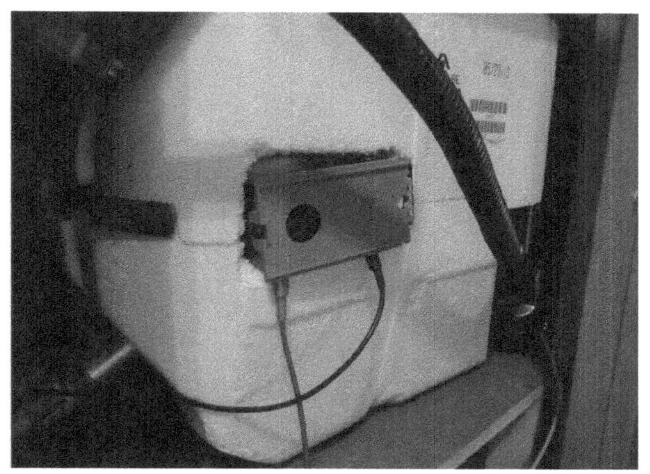

The switch wire was routed to the main control panel and switch installed. Then it was a simple task of plugging in the color coded wires and connecting the electricity.

New Water Heater Switch

If you look hard you can just make out the junction box where I was able to pull power. Luck was with me here or the install might have taken longer.

Adjustable Thermostat

This upgrade is so easy it will take longer to open the package with the part than do the upgrade. The same buddy that asked for the electric conversion also had the complaint that his gas water heater produced water that was too hot. An RV water heater has a fixed thermostat set at 140 degrees Fahrenheit. If you don't like this you are not stuck as Atwood makes a variable thermostat. Simply remove the fixed thermostat and replace with this one. The instructions

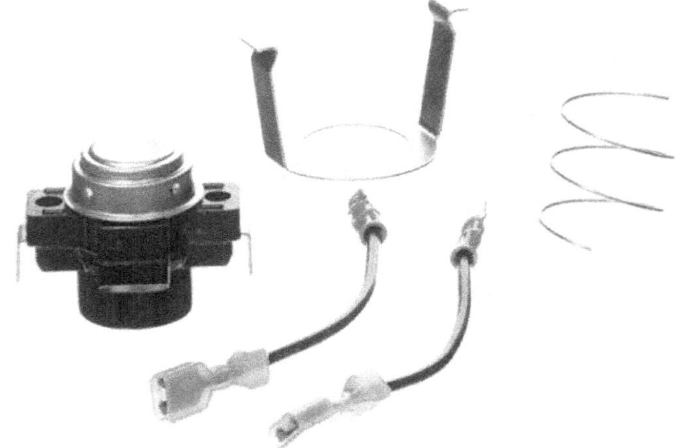

are very clear and it only takes a minute. You will then have an adjustment. The only down side is there is no gauge so it is trial and error to achieve the desired water temperature. Cost is less than $30.00.

https://www.amazon.com/Atwood-93105-Adjustable-Electronic-Thermostat/dp/B001BZ36HM/ref=sr_1_1?ie=UTF8&qid=1544232290&sr=8-1&keywords=atwood+93105+adjustable+electronic+thermostat

Cut the paper cover, remove original thermostat and replace with variable thermostat

I know that the title of the book is "My Best RV DIY Projects" but I had worked this up last year and decided to add it for fun. There are some good ideas I had not thought of that you may find useful.

 Every spring as you walk through Wal-Mart, the dollar stores, and even grocery stores what colorful item is seen in abundance? Pool Noodles. I thought it might be fun to see how creative campers have adapted these wiggle foam items for use in their RVs. The best part of this topic is that it can be told with pictures rather than words.

Inside the RV to hold the refrigerator door open when in storage and protect the glass turn table of the microwave.

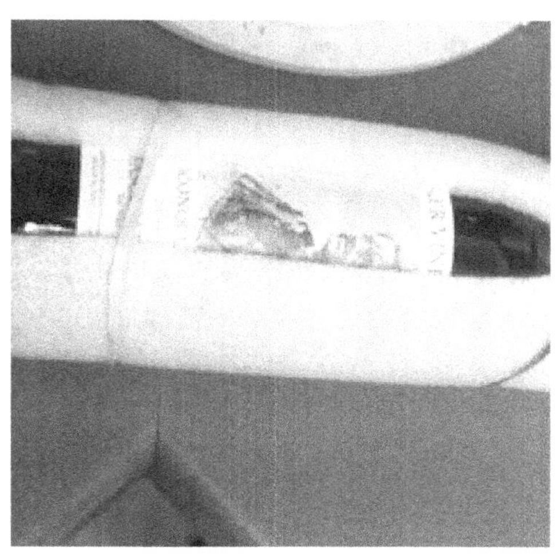 

Outside the RV as protection from snags, sharp corners or a rain gutter.

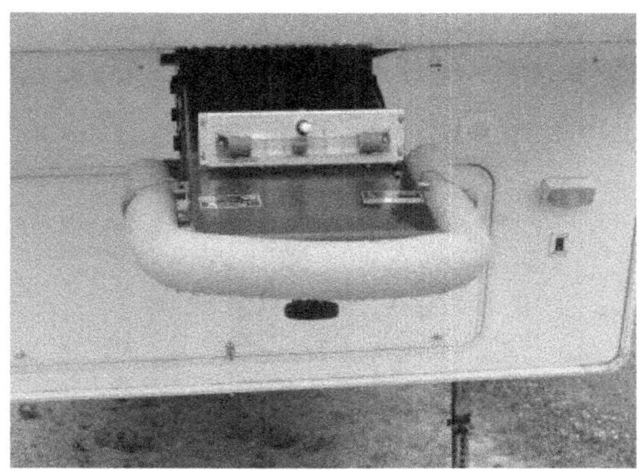 

 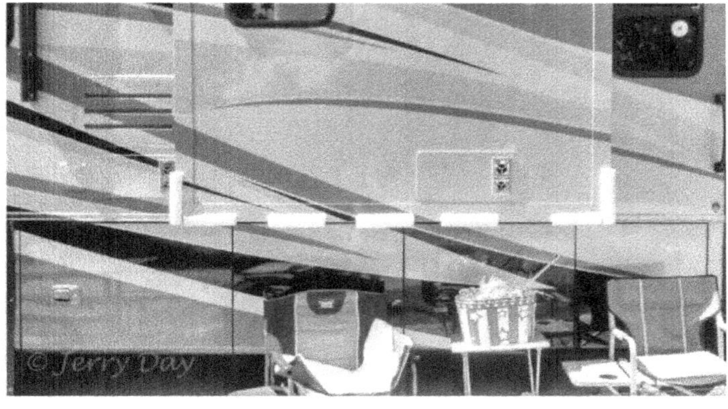

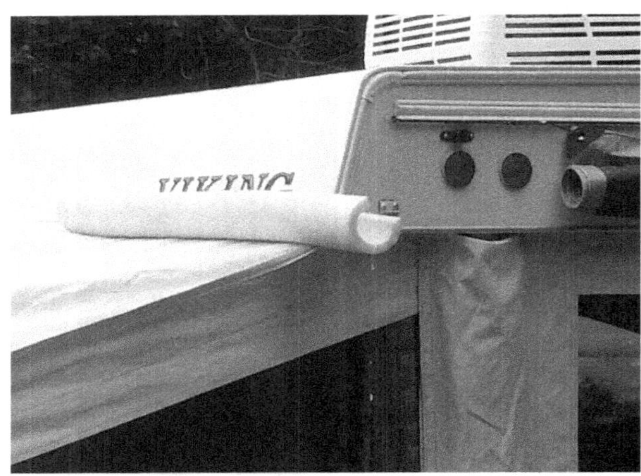

At the pool

Adapted for games

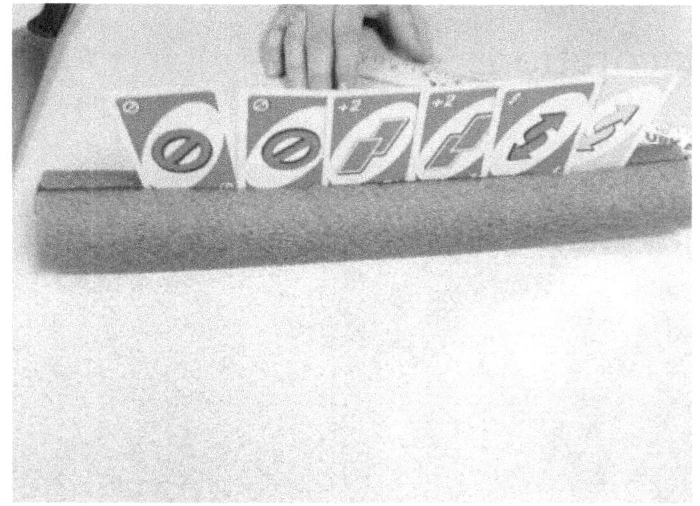

For decorations

Other uses

Thanks again for buying my book and supporting my efforts to bring you interesting RV topics. Until next time, happy RVing!